I0214424

BAD ASS WOMEN OF CINEMA

A COLLECTION OF INTERVIEWS
BY
CHRIS WATSON

BearManor
Media

Albany, Georgia

Bad Ass Women of Cinema: A Collection of Interviews

Copyright © 2015 Chris Watson. All Rights Reserved.

No part of this book may be reproduced in any form or by any means, electronic, mechanical, digital, photocopying or recording, except for the inclusion in a review, without permission in writing from the publisher.

Published in the USA by
BearManor Media
P.O. Box 71426
Albany, GA 31708
www.BearManorMedia.com

Cover art created by Mark R. Kosobucki

ISBN: 978-1-59393-963-2

Printed in the United States of America

BAD ASS WOMEN OF CINEMA

A COLLECTION OF INTERVIEWS
BY
CHRIS WATSON

TABLE OF CONTENTS

SPECIAL THANKS TO:

A big thank you to Henry and Elaine Watson, Brad Paulson, Eric Spudic, Len Kabasinski, Steve Carver, Lauren Nelsen, Jack Messitt, Jennifer Merecki, Ben Ohmart, Nick "The Punisher" Phillips, Brian Wilson, Kentaro, and all the wonderful women who made this book possible.

Steve Carver directs Chuck Norris in *Lone Wolf McQuade* (1983). Photo courtesy of Steve Carver.

INTRODUCTION

IN THE EARLY 1970S, ROGER CORMAN WAS MAKING MOVIES THAT exploited the popular fascination with the "girl gang" genre. He was the first post-war American filmmaker to break with the stereotyped image of woman as virgin, spouse, or femme fatale in popular pictures. His movies had an irresistible grip and desire sensitively attuned to the allure of the provocative and melodramatic tastes.

Women action movies were not without precedent. Women prisoners had been a marketable entertainment commodity since Lina Basquette was DeMille's *Godless Girl* in 1928, and Sylvia Sidney spent half the 1930s in celluloid lockup. Then the genre got its second wind with Corman. Oddly enough, the feminist movement greatly affected the consciousness of the filmmakers. Feminism and the exploitation of feminism proceeded coincidentally.

Girl gang action exploits feminism and is a metaphor for it. The only convincing feminist theatrical releases produced in Hollywood at the time were made by the low-budget exploitation industry due to the rest of the industries having abandoned feminism as un-exploitable after just a few lame attempts like *One is a Lonely Number* (1972) and *Stand Up and Be Counted* (1972).

When Corman re-entered the women action market in 1972 with *The Big Doll House*, he discovered that for a very low figure he could make a picture that appealed to the same audience that was supporting black action thrillers, as well as his standard audience of teenagers in drive-ins and lustful men. There were phenomenal savings to be made in production costs by shooting women action in the Philippines—a lesson later learned by other independent film companies.

The ingredients for success, which had since been repeated in every Corman-New World, American International, Dimension, and Crown International girl gang production, was tough talk and rough humor, glimpses of skin and sex, blood, gore and guts, chains, and hot clothing that gets ripped off. These exploitable feminism pictures posed rebellious goals like abstract liberty and pursuit in the most adventurists, reactionary, and forceful manner. Strenuous action, usually in pursuit of revenge, violating their violator or liberty from prison was in the mix too.

As a Corman protégé, I had the good fortune to direct two girl gang movies for Roger in the early 1970s: *The Arena* (1974) and *Big Bad Mama* (1974). The making of *The Arena* was supposed to be quick as well as cheap, with a shooting schedule of three or four weeks and another month to edit, add music and get the movie into theaters in order to give Corman a quick return on his investment. Unfortunately, it did not happen that way. After months of escalating production and location costs, and squabbles with producers in Israel and then in Spain, I finally began pre-production in Italy with Mark Damon, Roger's acting friend, producing the picture.

The Arena is a girl-gang epic starring Pam Grier and Margaret Markov, the only American women cast in the picture, re-teaming them from Corman's *Black Mama, White Mama* (1973). The movie stole movie bits from *Spartacus* (1960) and *The Defiant Ones* (1958), and was billed as "Black Slave, White Slave—See Wild Women Fight to the Death!" An action-packed saga of ancient Rome, it featured beautiful female gladiators who fought for their lives in the coliseum, cheered on by bloodthirsty Roman mobs. Those gladiators who escape death are forced to share the beds of their tyrannical masters. But in a stunning finale, the girls finally rebel against their fate, slaying their oppressors and fleeing through the ancient catacombs to freedom.

Grier, who was an attractive, large-busted, striking screen presence, had made fourteen movies in three years, mostly for Roger, and had become one of the most reliable B-movie stars in motion pictures. She and Victoria Principal would become the only veterans to make a break from the anonymity of the women-gang action pictures. Her name above the title was a smashing success for New World Pictures. Perhaps it was that success with audiences, coupled with the tedium of doing the same picture over and over again for the same limited audience, that moved Corman to experiment with larger budgets and drawing power of stars in women action. The use of a star also facilitated the shift from a gang action focus to character development—an important improvement in the two-year-old genre.

An unabashedly unpretentious picture with all the sex and violence an R-rating can sustain, *Big Bad Mama* was conceived as a hard-sell exploitation action comedy. Roger cast Angie Dickinson to play a tough, intelligent, aggressive pistol-packing mother of an all-girl band of robbers and kidnappers—the first movie to exploit the public's fascination with the Patty Hearst affair. He also hired William Shatner and Tom

Skerritt in supporting roles, actors with considerable drawing power from television and feature films.

A widowed mother of two teenaged, uninhibited nubile Lolitas, Dickinson enters a life of crime when a bootlegging uncle is shot and after she had decided that her daughters deserve a better life than dust bowl depression poverty. Reminiscent of *Bonnie and Clyde* (1967), *Big Bad Mama*'s plot and tone depicts mother and daughters quickly graduating to robbing banks with the experience of Skerritt and hindrance of Shatner, while retaining an unobtrusive underlying level of social protest. Forming a perversely appealing family-gang, Dickinson is spirited, sexy and gives a vivid, sympathetic and raucous performance as a woman motivated by mother love above all else but who is not averse to having some fun for herself.

Filmed entirely on colorful, authentic locations, from the first shot in Temecula, California, to general release in the U.S., it took only twelve weeks. Evoking the era on a slender budget, the crew was largely non-union, a Corman money-saver. The pay was lower than scale, the pace was quicker than normal, and the crew was younger. There were those that praise Roger for what he was doing for a lot of unknowns who lacked experience, saying that he was giving them a break. But the obverse of that is also true: he was exploiting much cheaper labor.

There is no doubt that *The Arena* and *Big Bad Mama* are cheap genre movies, slam bang pictures, which met their market head on. They proved, as if proof was needed, that the most exploitable here-today-gone-tomorrow genre—the girl gang movie—is the focus of really imaginative screen work in the underground of the commercial film industry.

Although actresses such as Pam Grier, Margaret Markov, and Angie Dickinson were breaking ground in the 1970s, it wasn't until the mid-1980s when Sigourney Weaver took on the acid-blooded alien in *Aliens* (1986) that women stopped being the objects of desire or the manipulative bitches, the helpless victims or sexy seductresses, and began to take leading roles in action pictures, kicking ass just as well as the greatest

Steve Carver on set with actor David Carradine.
Photo courtesy of Steve Carver.

male action heroes. The floodgates opened, and women have been wasting bad guys with guns and fists ever since.

The rise in women taking on roles that had traditionally been the exclusive property of male actors mirrored similar trends in society. Media portrayals follow societal changes, though not always with great accuracy, and we are seeing more active female characters on television programs and in films, as more women in the real world moved into traditionally male-identified roles.

However, since most movies are made by men, who aren't exactly renowned for their nuanced, complex understanding of female characters, it is easier to create female characters who function as window dressing—girlfriends, companions, and wives who tag along in the chase scenes, preferably screaming and falling down a lot, getting kidnapped at the climax, and disrobing for the sex scene. In theory, women action heroes break that mold. Movie audiences are drawn to or are intrigued by female action heroes because, in part, they run counter to the norm. We are inundated with images of male protagonists, so it's refreshing to see women lead, and, of course, run around kicking ass and shooting things.

As a culture, we still have a difficult time figuring out how to react to these strong women. Although women are achieving numerical equality, there are key differences between the women and their male sparring partners. Female characters who act in heroic ways are still held to a higher and more unrealistic appearance standard than their male counterparts. They are often placed in a classic double bind: if they are powerful, they may be perceived as more masculine and thus threaten the social order; if they are more traditionally feminine, they are deemed socially acceptable but also less powerful.

In any discussion of female role models in a visual medium like film, body image issues are unavoidable. Female action heroes go a long way in showcasing the wonder and might of female physical power by going against the grain of Hollywood's current standard of beauty, which implicitly prizes physical weakness via the super-thin bodies of most young actresses.

One of the most frequent arguments against female action movies is that female stars can't "open" action movies. Action movies are geared primarily at an audience of teenage boys—a crowd not known for their keen appreciation of the female psyche. In this testosterone-driven market, they won't go and see female action movies, even with guns and explosions—it's still a "chick flick."

And then, there is a misconception about action heroines in general. We tend to think that action heroines are breaking down gender barriers and that they are empowering role models, especially for young women. The action heroines really do not draw upon any form of feminine power but act in ways similar to their male counterparts who are heightened versions of ideals and traits men are already supposed to aspire to, such as strength, decisiveness, acting as protectors. They take on male-affiliated traits and then heighten them.

Female action heroes are positive, inspirational figures because audiences want to see more female protagonists distinguished by their heart, courage, and smarts—role model attributes. Strength and protectiveness, qualities that don't belong solely to men, make more thoughtful movies about what femininity brings to the table in fraught situations, and it is far more interesting storytelling with nuanced role models.

—*Steve Carver*

Bridget (Rebekah Brandes) goes head to head with Radford in Jack Messitt's *Midnight Movie*. Photo courtesy of Jack Messitt.

REBEKAH
BRANDES

REBEKAH BRANDES IS YOUNG, BUT SHE HAS ALREADY FOUND SUCCESS in a modern-day film career. Rebekah began in the micro-budget Troma film *Slaughter Party* (2005), which features Felissa Rose and Brinke Stevens. She followed up *Slaughter Party* with the European horror film *Evil Ever After* (2006). She took a step up by appearing in the higher-budget films *Succubus: Hell Bent* (2007) and *Grim Reaper* (2007) before landing the lead role in the theatrical release *Midnight Movie* (2008). Brandes guest-starred on the television shows *Greek*, *NCIS*, and the pilot for *The Forgotten*, but at this point she hadn't received the role that would allow her to break out.

Surprisingly, Rebekah Brandes found success by returning to micro films with a supporting role in *Bellflower* (2011). John Anderson of *Variety* wrote, "the performers are all good, notably the promising Rebekah Brandes as Courtney, sort of a nymphet with a .45." The success of *Bellflower* has allowed Brandes to work steadily in higher-budget films, including *April Apocalypse* (2013) and *Nothing Left to Fear* (2013). Although her career is in the beginning stages, Rebekah Brandes has proven to be filled with talent and potential, playing many unforgettable and strong characters.

Notable roles
Midnight Movie
Bellflower
Evil Ever After

Chris: How would you describe your childhood?

Rebekah: My childhood was dysfunctional, for sure, but incredibly exciting in a lot of ways. I had three brothers, and we're all close to the same age, so I had a pack of boys around me at all times. That made me kind of a guy's girl. We moved around to several different places growing up. I was constantly switching schools and moving, but I was a shy, sensitive kid. That was all very visceral. My parents were incredibly intense, passionate people who had us when they were very young. We all love each other very much, but we're all intense. My parents were both different personalities. My mom was always into music. They had a lot of opinions, were very into arts and crafts, talking, and discussing. My childhood was jam-packed with life-shaping experiences.

Chris: What inspired you to become an actress?

Rebekah: My earliest memory of acting was probably at five. I was outside at a party, goofing around and having fun. One of the adult guests laughed at me and said, "You're an entertainer." That was the first time I thought about it. That was very meaningful and kind of clicked even at that young age.

My favorite teacher ever, Mrs. Baker, told me I was going to be in the school play. I was in the third grade, so we didn't audition or anything, she just said, "You're going to be the lead." I was the Queen of Sheba. I loved to be on stage. That's who I am. After that, I was always in acting classes and Community Theater. Age eight is when I decided to move to Hollywood. I was really proud that I went through with it ten years later.

Chris: You found out at the read through for *Slaughter Party* that the killer was a dwarf. How did this change your view of the movie?

Rebekah: When I found out the killer was a dwarf, I got immensely more excited. It was my first film in Los Angeles, so I was already excited. I thought, "I'm in LA, filming a movie, and I'm going to get killed by a dwarf. This is surreal." Exciting and surreal are good words to describe it. I was a little disturbed too—in a good way.

Chris: The girls in *Slaughter Party* physically give it their all. What are some physical challenges you faced on the film?

Rebekah: I had a really amazing time making that film. The running around on the rocks and the rolling around on the gravel with Mighty Mike on top of me was a physical challenge. To be honest, I feel like I've had worse experiences on other films. When I was running barefoot, I was worried I would eat shit and tumble all over the rocks and Mighty Mike would fall on top of me, giving a real bloodbath. Luckily, it went well and was fun.

Chris: You told me before your displeasure with being in multiple mainstream films with adult stars. Can you elaborate on that?

Rebekah: With the internet these days, I used to Google my name, and the first five results that came up were "Rebekah Brandes and Ron Jeremy." I didn't even realize we were in a few different films together. We never shot together. My parents or whoever would Google me were seeing my name with Ron Jeremy. It is not the sort of thing you want on the internet, but I can handle it. Ron Jeremy's an esteemed actor. I am sorry I never got to meet him.

Chris: He has done good movies, though, like *Boondock Saints* (1999)...

Rebekah: He's okay. It's just his name coming up. I didn't think about the internet-movie-database factor. I didn't know he was in *Slaughter Party*. Is he even in *Slaughter Party*?

Chris: He makes a tacked-on cameo. I remember you had shot *Curse of Pirate Death* (2006) and found out Ron was in it on the set of *Evil Ever After*. You freaked out a little.

Rebekah: Yeah, I did. Even though he only had a cameo in *Slaughter Party*, his name was already connected to mine. Then he was in another movie with me. I thought, "This is it. For the rest of time, I'm going to be associated with Ron Jeremy's name." I thought it was all over, but it worked out. You can't find the names together now unless you try.

Chris: Because of the speed of the deal, *Evil Ever After* was being written while it was shot. How did this complicate things for you as an actress?

Rebekah: I think it made it easier because I got a fresh day every day. I got more of an organic experience. To not know what was going to happen was interesting. With the character, I know what her core was. I liked having direction on the day more than knowing exactly what was going to happen.

Chris: Your character is very strong even though she's sick in the head. What did you see as leading to her breakdown in your death scene?

Rebekah: She took it too far, got overwhelmed with her power, and got what was coming to her because she was getting out of control. She was very strong. It was definitely a turnaround but more of a collapse. She had an epic moment beating up that poor guy, but it all came crashing down around her soon enough.

Chris: You worked with Felissa Rose and Brinke Stevens in these films. What did you think about working with such iconic, cult actresses?

Rebekah: I knew of Felissa from *Sleepaway Camp* (1983). I knew they were huge horror icons before working with them. Felissa was amazingly nice and beautiful on *Slaughter Party*. It was inspiring to see someone who's an icon be so sweet and having a very good time on such a low- budget film. She was very positive all of the time. I see both of their pictures on all of these horror sites. It was definitely great to be associated with them.

Chris: Before *Bellflower*, it looked like your career was going in a similar direction by being in so many horror films. Were you ever concerned about that?

Rebekah: Yes, I was. I was concerned about it because I wanted to do a variety of movies. Horror is addicting because it's a guilty pleasure for acting too. The films are oftentimes awful, but there are a lot of fans. It's easy to get into that whole scene. For a short time I was concerned, but I decided to embrace it. Why shouldn't I be a horror film actress? Maybe I could be a scream queen. That would be fun. At first, I wanted to do other acting roles and not the formulaic horror film again and again. Now, I know there are amazing horror films out there. You don't always have to follow the same path. It's not something I worry about anymore. Someone in a review called me a "scream queen vet." It's a huge compliment.

Chris: On *Evil Ever After*, you were uncomfortable with kissing scenes. Were your scenes in *Succubus* difficult in the same way?

Rebekah: God yes. It's been about five years and I'm just starting to become comfortable with love scenes. (In *Succubus*) I sit in boy-shorts and a bra, with a girl in a thong and a guy with no shirt on. That was uncomfortable. I've realized the love scenes are just going to become more and more intense. I just went into an audition where I'm supposed to jump on a guy, straddle him, start kissing his neck, and tell him I wanted to fuck him next to his dead mom. I just went for it. It was actually really fun. Once I realized they were going to get either grittier or more intimate, I got over it. With *Succubus: Hell Bent*, though, I was an eighteen-year-old and very uncomfortable.

I remember (on *Evil Ever After*), I just had to make out with him while wearing a bikini top, right?

Chris: Yes.

Rebekah: I was so young then. I didn't realize what the industry would do to me. Now I'm just like, "You want me to take my top off? I'll take it off." (Laughs)

Chris: Knowing how uncomfortable you were with love scenes, did you ever think that when you did nudity it would be on such a low-budget film?

Rebekah: I didn't get involved with *Bellflower* in the traditional way. I'd worked with, and been friends, with them at that point. We all hung out, would go drinking together, and make little movies together. I went to acting school with Tyler Dawson. I'm pretty sure when Evan asked me to be in it I asked, "I don't have to do any nudity, right?" He said, "Of course not." Then we're on set at 4 a.m. in Ventura on some random day, and he said, "Oh, by the way, we realized we can't really have you in a t-shirt in the bed. You have to be topless. It won't fit with the rest of the movie."

At that point, they had already filmed some very explicit scenes with Jessie Wiseman, and the tone and style of the movie was becoming very real and gritty. I believed in the movie so much, and couldn't justify not taking it off, as opposed to usually when I think, "Why am I taking my shirt off? Why would you want me to do that right now?" *Bellflower* is very gritty, beautiful, and real. It was right. It was weird because I said, "No nudity," for so long. In the end, I would just do anything on that set because it was an honor to be around those guys making that movie. At the time, it was like nothing I had done before. My character was different than anything I had ever done.

The first thing I thought about when Evan called me to tell me we were going to be in Sundance was, "Oh my God, my boobs are going to be at Sundance." I freaked out. That was huge. The one tiny movie I do nudity in goes to Sundance and gets seen by a bunch of people. It had to be done sooner or later, so I'm glad it's a movie that is considered an art film. It's hard to say "No," to Evan. It's such a passion piece.

Chris: What are your thoughts on micro films?

Rebekah: They're the best. If you can do a micro film and it's something people like, there's no better feeling. I think it's a really cool thing to do. All you have to rely on is your own skill set, creativity, passion, and team of people. A huge plus for me is that they're usually way less professional on set. I'm not a professional person. It feels way more involved and exciting. Even if I film something with a really low budget and it's being shot on a little digital camera, it can still be a really cool experience. You can go places and get fans. The first fan letters I got were not for my big-budget films, but they were from fans of *Slaughter Party* and *Evil Ever After*. Those didn't need a big budget but a lot of passion. You can't ask for any more validation or proof that you are doing the art because you didn't use anything but art to make it.

Chris: Do you feel that the success of *Bellflower* changed that perspective any?

Rebekah: I've always had that perspective. There are different kinds of micro films. I always liked micro films more. I didn't think they were going to be as successful as I now realize they can be. I filmed *Bellflower* two years ago. I filmed a web series a few months before that. I really like the small, creative sets instead of huge, scary sets. I would have to do a lot more big-budget stuff if I want to be a working actor. That's why I'm so happy that the micro budget one is the one that paid off the biggest for me, so far. It's very validating that I haven't been wasting my time or money working for free.

Micro films allow way more control and power. Obviously, the money and stuff is nice on bigger-budget projects. A lot of micro films are more fun to watch than the big-budget ones. The stuff people are making for the internet are so much more fun to film, be around, and watch. Anybody can get a camera and make it look good now. You don't have to be good at filmmaking. The technology is more available, making it more competitive.

Chris: Your character in *Grim Reaper* is very weak. If you were able to rewrite the script, what would change about her?

Rebekah: I would have calmed her down. She was always freaking out, and it wasn't helping anyone. She was a very sensitive person, but she was young. I think she was supposed to be fourteen in that movie. She wasn't a strong character. At the end, in the generator room, she got a little stronger.

Rebekah Brandes in Jack Messitt's *Midnight Movie*.
Photo courtesy of Jack Messitt.

Chris: Describe for me how you view your character's transformation in *Midnight Movie*.

Rebekah: In *Midnight Movie*, I think Bridget goes from a hardened, bitter, held-back girl who's on the defense at all times, to someone who has to put herself totally out there, realizing feeling fear is something you have to get over. Before that, she doesn't want to deal with anything. She's very closed off in the beginning. By the end, she realizes what she has to do to get her brother out of there alive is to put herself out there. She has to go to a place and let her guard down. That's the only way to get through the killer's shell and get on the same level. She got vulnerable, which made her stronger in the end. I think she was a little repressed and had to go all out to save the day—and she did.

Chris: Describe for me your experience with *Bellflower* getting into the Sundance Film Festival.

Rebekah: It was insane. I had been talking to Evan every six months for the past two years. I would Facebook him, seeing what was up with the movie. They had been working on it for two years straight. I was basically, "Damn, that movie won't come out." I really wanted it to. I knew it was going to look cool, but I was over it. Then, I got a message from Evan saying, "Call me. I have big news." I thought, "Oh, God, it's probably the Medusa car got a new blower or something about the car or needing to do a pick up shot." I didn't call him for like two days. Then I got three messages from the rest of them saying, "Call Evan." I couldn't think of one thing that would be that exciting. I hadn't even seen the movie. When he told me it was going to Sundance, I was like, "Oh, cool. Oh, ok..." In a ninety-second span I went from ten to a hundred, screaming, as it sank in. It was a big shock. It was the best time of my life, so far. The happiness of getting to go there with everyone was amazing. He always said he wanted to get into Sundance, but every film you make at this level wants to do the festival circuit. I'm always, "Sure you are." But he actually took us to Sundance, and it was by far one of the best experiences in my life.

Chris: What do you think would have happened to the film if it hadn't gotten in?

Rebekah: I think about it every day. Where would it be right now? Evan was so obsessed with it that it never would've gone away. I know Evan submitted it on a whim on the last day you could submit. I'd like to think he'd just keep submitting it to other things and working on it. If nothing happened, he'd start another movie. *Bellflower* may not have happened, but maybe the next one would have happened. I didn't really expect it to get into Sundance. Everything would be different right now, but I believe he would've made another film.

Chris: How would you describe your character in *Bellflower*?

Rebekah: My character gets to be the dark horse. She starts out really sweet and shy. By the end, she's at the other end of the spectrum. She's got a gun in her purse, and the movie gets surreal. I got to have three different fight scenes. I'm pretty bad ass by the end. I grab this one chick by the hair and slam the door on another one's face. That was fun.

In the end, she kills herself rather than the guy. She's bad ass, but she doesn't seem to have her priorities figured out. She doesn't know where to direct her good traits. First of all, by the end of the movie, she's a figment of a guy's imagination. However, she's bad ass; she gets a gun, and she does what she wants. She's definitely got power.

Chris: You've had a lot of success where others have failed. What has your approach been towards your career?

Rebekah: It wasn't a choice. I came here to spend the rest of my life making movies. The big difference between me and other actors I know, is that to them it's more of a plan. If it doesn't work, then they go back to Minnesota or Washington or wherever. They make dream poster boards and lists of goals. I never really had a plan. I came here for the long haul. When I got here, the plan was to be here and make it in Hollywood. I'm such a moment to moment person, and I think that's the biggest difference.

Acting wise, I do what I want. I'm serious about it. I think a lot of people just aren't as passionate as they need to be. Some people work harder, go to more auditions, spend more man hours, but I think it's more that this is what I do. That's the biggest thing I've noticed is that they're more result oriented. I'm also just a lucky girl.

Harrison Ford said he was the only one of his friends left out here when he made it. You also have to put in the years. The way you look at it will reflect in your acting. For me, I didn't spend hours writing down my goals. Instead, I tried to be what I wanted to be. Don't think about it. You just have to be it. I don't know if that would work if I were someone else or doing it at some other time, but that's how I feel. Everybody's different. I know a lot of talented, passionate actors and nothing happens. I've got a little guilt about having a little success because it's so hard. I feel guilty. Then, I see some other actor making millions for some crappy film, and I don't feel guilty anymore—I get bitter.

Chris: There's an interview you did where the interviewer was doing their best to try to pull something negative out of you, but you remained a class act. Would you say this is intentional or natural?

Rebekah: It was natural. I'm not really intentional. I am a "say whatever the hell I want to say at all times" kind of person. When people ask me how I feel, I tell them how I feel. If I felt negative, I would have said something negative. I don't do things that I don't want to do. I don't pretend to do things that I didn't do. I'm proud of everything and happy with how my life and career has turned out. Nobody interviewing me could ever get me to say something negative about acting, movies, Hollywood, or anything I've been in. This is my career and life. If I was going to say something negative, what the hell would be the point of being here? When it comes to movies there's no negativity from me. A lot of people out there don't know themselves or what to do. I knew what I was doing when I made these movies. I was happy as fuck to be there. I'm not the type that is going to look back six years later, "What the hell did I do?!" If you know what you're doing, you can't complain about the experience. I came out here to have fun and do what I want to do, so it'd be silly to trash on the movies and people who made that possible. I'll always remember those movies. I still remember the first time we filmed a scene on *Slaughter Party,* where we're all sitting around the car. I remember noticing the camera was on me. I was so excited in my head, but I was terrified on set.

Chris: Have you ever reconsidered your career as an actress?

Rebekah: No. I've gotten scared. "Am I going to be able to survive?" "This is horrible." But did I ever think, "Am I going to have to go back to school?" No. I'll either have to be working as an actor or I'll have to get married and have babies. Then, I'd be an actor in my spare time. I know that sounds horrible, but there's no other job for me. If I have to revert to anything, it'll be to my nature-given role as a child bearer.

Chris: What do you look up to in other actresses?

Rebekah: I look up to the actresses who do what they want to do. They do them regardless of what they're supposed to do based on how they look or sound. I can't wait to be able to write movies to make the roles I want to be in. There aren't very many roles for women that are based on being a woman. I want to be a pilot or a scientist, not the (stereotypical) woman role. I like actresses who don't follow gender roles. Leading ladies are great. Romantic interests are great, but I really admire character actresses and comedic actresses. I also really admire actresses who do the real, old-school acting work. I don't like the ones who are nineteen, doing a movie every three months because they're a product. I love the artists like Kate Winslet. I look up to actresses who respect the entire process. (I look up to) the ones who understand we are only one element of it and not the whole movie. They appreciate how much work goes into it. If I like a movie I'm in, it's an honor to be in that movie, and it should be an honor for them to have you in that movie too. I like the actresses who are more collaborative. Sometimes they might have a bad movie come out. I like Jennifer Aniston, she's a good actress, but she doesn't take any risks anymore. I respect actresses who don't worry about the results. They do it because they have to and want to.

Chris: What do you feel makes a strong female character?

Rebekah: It should be a well-rounded character that has nothing to do with her as a woman any more than a man's character has to do with him being a man. Strong female characters are women who do what they want, know what they want, and know who they are. I feel like a lot of movies depict women not knowing what they want, they don't figure it out until the very end, and then they're "Oh, this is what I wanted—a man!" I like women characters who are fully developed people from the beginning of the movie. They're normal people with full arcs, transitions, and things that are related to the world and not just their heart, their man, and their body. Women who think about other issues are an example. I don't think it has to be a tough woman. I think it's more about a woman character that could be a man or a woman. They are just a strong person.

Chris: Who do you consider to be a Bad Ass Woman of Cinema and why?

Rebekah: I would say Kate Winslet for many reasons. Kate's bad ass because she's a great example of a beautiful woman who's not quite the leading-lady type but still succeeds in playing great roles. I remember hearing how she got the role in *Titanic* (1997) because they didn't want to cast her. She sent a rose to James Cameron and kept at it. She had the most passion. Kate did the role wonderfully. Then she goes on to do all of these incredible movies. Eventually, she even plays a Nazi pedophile. She does exactly what she wants acting wise and isn't limited to romantic leads. She's also really funny in *Extras*. She has shown she has an amazing sense of humor and can make fun of herself. She's natural looking still. Even though she's beautiful and sexual, she's not a sex symbol but an actor. That's what I really like about her. She can do it all. She's just the coolest.

Sophia Crawford in action!
Photo courtesy of Sophia Crawford.

SOPHIA
CRAWFORD

SOPHIA CRAWFORD'S TRAGIC TEENAGE YEARS WOULD CHANGE THE course of her life forever. Following the death of her mother, Sophia and her sister backpacked across Asia. Sophia began modeling for print ads, picking up odd jobs that eventually led to small roles in movies. She moved to Hong Kong and took on some of Cinema's toughest ladies, including Moon Lee and Yukari Oshima. Sophia was often cast as the Caucasian villain who the audience was glad to see get clobbered or killed in arguably the most vicious female fights ever put to film. The Hong Kong films would introduce Sophia to both martial arts and stunt work, including training with Yukari's Funky Action Crew. Sophia made around thirty action films during the infamous "Girls with Guns" period, before moving to America. Hollywood offered Sophia the opportunity to utilize the skills she picked up in Hong Kong—martial arts, weapons training, stunts, and acting experience. Sophia appears in supporting roles in films like *U.S. Seals 2* (2001), but she also made a career of stunt work for TV and film. Sophia has worked consistently in various facets of film, proving over and over again that she's tough as they get.

Notable roles
Beauty Investigator
Angel Terminators 2
Buffy the Vampire Slayer
Cyprus Tigers

Chris: What function did your travels play in your future career?
Sophia: My travels played an enormous role in my career. I don't think I would have accomplished anything if I had not left. I wouldn't have been a stuntwoman or any of these things I became later on if I hadn't got off my butt and headed for Asia. When I left England, it was a very tricky time for me. I don't want to go into any details, but it was very difficult growing up. Yes, many families are dysfunctional, and I am not passing blame to anyone. I was a very reckless teenager who rebelled. I was extremely angry and got expelled from five different schools for fighting and truancy. Eventually, there were no schools that would take me, and it's not something I am proud of. The Kent County Council ordered a taxi to pick me up at my house and drive me to the vicarage three times a week. The vicar's wife tutored me there privately until I was sixteen. She would try to teach me, but at that time I was a bit of a lost cause. I failed the only two exams I took, and I felt my life was going downhill pretty quickly. When I realized I had failed my education, I really didn't know which direction to turn. My sister, Ingrid, and I just said, "Let's go." It was an impulsive thing to do. We didn't make a big plan ahead of time; we saw an ad in a magazine and simply decided to go for it. Before we knew it, we

were on a bus with our tent and two backpacks, heading for Asia. I had no idea that I was going to go away and not come back. Initially, our plan was to go for six months, straighten out our heads, and find some sort of work in England when we returned, even though I knew prospects were severely grim. I wanted to go to Asia. I wanted to run away and think about what I wanted to be. I felt so compelled to leave England but didn't really understand why. As we started this journey overland to India, my sister and I discovered we both had a love for travel. We were meeting a lot of interesting people and going to many new countries, having so many exciting experiences that we couldn't possibly go back home to stay. When we got to Thailand, my sister said to me, "I want to go to South America." I said, "I don't. I love Thailand. I want to stay here." We popped home very briefly, dumped our backpacks, said "Happy Birthday," to our Dad and then separated. Ingrid went to South America, and I flew back to Thailand on my own in search of something. I felt a very strong affection for the country and its people. I didn't know exactly what I was searching for, but I knew this was where I wanted to begin.

Chris: You began your film career in Thailand.

Sophia: I knew I needed a job, so I got one at the Central Plaza Hotel in Bangkok. My job was to teach the staff English. The hotel gave me a modeling assignment, which was a small brochure. After that, the agency that got me that job asked me if I wanted to be an extra in an American production called *Kickboxer* (1989) with Jean Claude Van Damme. They were looking for Caucasians to be in a bar and fill up the background. I was always very sociable. I loved talking to the crew and everybody, so I got to chatting. One guy said, "Why do you want to do movies in Thailand? You're not going to be able to do movies in Thailand. You are British; you have a British passport don't you? Why don't you go and work in Hong Kong?" Bingo! I could work in Hong Kong without worrying about a special visa. In Thailand, I was having a tough time getting my work permit, and I had to work illegally. I didn't want to do that. I wanted to do it right. I also wanted to work in films where I could speak English and communicate better with people on the streets. So, I went to Hong Kong. I knew nothing about the whole Hong Kong movie craze. I didn't know that there were people watching Hong Kong movies back home because that's not how I grew up. I didn't grow up watching a lot of television. I grew up running through the fields. I was a tomboy who was outdoors playing with my sisters all the time. Right from the beginning, the Hong Kong experience was a new one to me. It took time to figure out who was who, where the stunt team came from and how they trained. A lot of my training was done on camera. I would've loved to have had some martial arts skills in my pocket before I arrived but I didn't. I threw myself into the fire, and just said, "Hey guys, I really want to do this. I really want to learn. Can you teach me?" And they did.

Chris: How did you finally become involved in martial arts?

Sophia: I began training with the stunt guys in Hong Kong. There were several excellent western martial arts guys working there at the time but no women. There was a void of women, but there was a call for women. They needed western women to beat up! I was very willing to learn something new, so I practiced martial arts, gymnastics and stunts with the Hong Kong stunt guys plus a few of the local westerners. I would often train in Kowloon Park with Rambo Kong or in the gym with Michiko Nishiwaki. Occasionally, I would train a little with Gary Chow in his class. I started learning fighting skills for camera. It began there, but I also had the opportunity to train with Yukari Oshima when I joined her stunt team. Her background was in karate and stunts. She was fierce on screen, and I loved her intensity. I learned a lot from Yukari, and she became my mentor and manager. When I came to the states I started training in Tae Kwon Do at Jun Chong's and then at Simon Rhee's school for several years. My husband Jeff Pruitt has also influenced me over the years in stunts and martial arts.

Chris: What did you learn from Yukari?

Sophia: Yukari taught me about intensity. She showed me how to use acted–power and expression in my fights. We had very few "actual" conversations. She didn't speak very good English and my Cantonese was pretty poor. It didn't matter because we were able to get along on a level that didn't require it. Sign language, laughter and a love of action was enough for us to have a mutual understanding. I had so much respect for her and her work. I really liked the way she applied herself on set. She was very professional, extremely tough, never complained and was not a diva. She inspired me in so many ways, and I will always be grateful to her.

Chris: Was it more difficult for your career being female or Caucasian?

Sophia: Both were difficult, as was being a martial artist at that time. The bar is set very high in Hong Kong, so being a white woman and being new to martial arts came with a huge amount of criticism. If you're going to take risks, you're going to take criticism. I had to take risks in a lot of what I did. I couldn't worry about whether I looked stupid or not. On the other hand, I would sometimes get compliments like "She's got heart." I think they respected that I wouldn't say "No," to anything. I would always give it my best shot. The only thing I would say about being white is that I felt racial tension towards me at times, but it was more off set than on. The changeover was happening with the British, and I was working as a model while trying to break into the film industry. When I had to go to an audition, I would sometimes doll-up a bit in skirts and high heels. I remember getting kicked in the street once by a man, saying, "Go back home!" There was that underlying tension towards me at times that I was different from anywhere else on my travels. I got lots of dirty looks and even spitting at me on occasion. It was always from the older generations. The younger kids didn't seem to care. I guess because they were already steeped in western culture. At night, I might go out with a group of people to a karaoke bar or something. Many business meetings took place in bars late at night. Everyone is having fun, being social, and then you arrive on set the next day and suddenly these same people are not talking to you. I would realize they're not "supposed" to talk to me, because I'm white. They follow along with the sheep. Behind closed doors, it was great and they were my "friends." Although it was transparent to me, I honestly didn't care. It wasn't going to stop me from chasing my dreams. I had a passion for action films, and I wanted to be part of it. I met many different kinds of people in Hong Kong. Some of them were amazing and others were not.

Chris: How do you think women are viewed in Asian cinema?

Sophia: That's a good question. It's changed, but has it changed? I came in during the "Girls with Guns" era. Several women were playing fierce characters onscreen, fighting just as hard as the guys. I was really impressed that women were allowed such tough roles. Later, the fad started to die and production slowed down. In many ways it was a great era because it gave a lot of girls strong leading roles. Yukari had a good run in these movies but later moved to the Philippines for a while because there were fewer roles in Hong Kong. At the time, she asked me to go with her and stay with her team, but I had decided to give Los Angeles a try. I felt that I couldn't progress any further in Hong Kong. The genre had changed into period and costume dramas and women had even less fighting roles—zero for white women like me. Maybe it's swinging back to where more women are featured again, but those "Girls with Guns" days are classic. We were working bare knuckles back then, using mattresses to land on and leather straps for harnesses. The riggers were using very thin cable to fly people, and it often broke. Many stuntmen got hurt during this time. If you were a member of either Jackie or Sammo's stunt team, you were taken care of. If not, then you were on your own. Some of the HKG stunt guys came to America and purchased all types of stunt equipment. They bought air bags, pads, flying harnesses and cable. Then they returned to Hong Kong with it, and eventually things evolved. Stunt safety is so much better now. It will never be the way it was back then.

Chris: Besides what we've discussed already, in what ways were you treated differently between American and Asian films?

Sophia: I had some great moments on set and met some really cool people while working in Hong Kong films. Sure, I had the odd incident here and there, but, on the whole, Hong Kong was a unique, once in a lifetime experience. The language barrier was difficult at times. It was very hard to find out what the scene was about and what I was supposed to do. Someone would hand me a piece of paper and then tell to me say some lines in Cantonese. I never saw a script. I got bits of information from ten different people using one-word commands like "Left, right, faster, harder!" In America, I would usually see a script. I'm not just being thrown in front of a camera.

Chris: Did you have any rules as to how your fights should go?

Sophia: I wasn't given many opportunities to voice what I wanted.

Chris: Would that be the same in both American and Asian films?

Sophia: It would depend on whom I was working for at the time. There are certain situations where you are simply not allowed to make a suggestion. Other times it's more of a team effort. Over the years, while working in America, I have worked with several different stunt coordinators who trust me and with whom I have built a rapport. It is these coordinators who may ask me to go choreograph a fight and bring it to them. We work together. When I was working in Hong Kong, I wouldn't have dared to make a suggestion. I was just a student trying to learn, and these guys were masters.

I have only done a few American films where I wasn't doubling someone. I had little to do with my choreography in any of them. I was a little disappointed with my fights in *Sword of Honor* (1996) because it was my first American film, and my expectations were higher. It was very low budget, and we shot most of it in Vegas. The producers cast two bodybuilders for me to fight with, and they had zero stunt experience. As a result, it was very difficult for them to sell a single reaction. Jeff and I were upset but had to deal with it. *U.S Seals 2* (2001) was an enjoyable movie, although I wasn't in brilliant physical condition at the time. Nevertheless, I got to do a little action, and it was a pleasure working for Isaac Florentine and Andy Cheng.

Chris: Do you prefer performing a fight scene with a male or female?

Sophia: I prefer a female if she hits hard. Seriously, though, I prefer multiple males or females. I like to fight a bunch of people at once—multiple opponents.

Chris: I'm going to give you a few names. Tell me about working with Gordon Liu.

Sophia: I absolutely love him. We were actually friends in Hong Kong. We hung out sometimes and had some great chats because his English was quite good. Really, I think he just liked to practice speaking English with me. He has a sweet heart and wasn't prejudice at all. He's a lovely, generous man.

Chris: Simon Yam.

Sophia: I was in love with Simon for years. At one time, I had a huge crush on him. I'm a big fan of his work, and I think he's a terrific actor. I loved working with him because he had a sense of humor!

Chris: Moon Lee.

Sophia: We started off on rough ground when I did my first film, *New Killers in Town* (1990). Moon got frustrated with me because I was brand new. I was trying to get through the choreography, and I kept making mistakes, so she kicked me in the throat. She didn't apologize and laughed about it. The crew followed suit, and pretty soon everyone was laughing at me. That just made me fight harder and probably got a better performance out of me. It was humiliating stuff like that that set a fire under my butt. You can humiliate me. I'll take it, but I'll just train harder and be better. The next few films that Moon and I did together she could see that I was progressing, training hard, and getting better. We started to fight better together, much more fluid. We weren't really good friends, but we were sociable and worked together well.

Chris: Do you prefer playing a heroine or villain?

Sophia: Villain. It's rougher around the edges. I'm not a clean-cut girl. I like to think I'm a kind person, though.

Chris: Talk about the fight scenes between you and Yukari. They are often very brutal and not what you would expect from a fight scene between women. They are always very fast, well-choreographed but brutal.

Sophia: Yukari is a bad ass. She was very powerful and stood out from the other women fighting in Hong Kong because of her skills and her spirit. She was an actress with the heart of a true stuntwoman. In Hong Kong action films you were expected to make a certain amount of contact when kicking and punching. The aim was not to hurt each other but emphasize speed and power. Thankfully, she was very good at controlling her kicks! I wanted the fights to be brutal, but that is what was so unique about Hong Kong action films at the time. The girls fought along with the guys and, in most cases, were just as tough. Yet, in the U.S, girls were still being towed by their male leads. Yukari was a legitimate fighter who knew exactly how to translate it to the big screen.

Chris: What do you think it takes to create a well-coordinated fight scene?

Sophia: I think it helps if you utilize the environment and keep the style of action right for the genre. Some films might have action, but it doesn't fit the script. Why does this guy have those kinds of powers when there's no reasoning for it? A good fight scene requires great camera angles, movement, fast-paced choreography, talented stunt performers and a lot of energy! It's not just about you. If you throw fast, hard punches, and the guy or girl you're hitting isn't doing solid reactions, then you're going to look weak. Also, the camera angle has to be right. A bad angle will reflect poorly on the stunt people or may not capture the stunt at all. All the departments have to work together. When it all works, it's a beautiful thing.

Chris: In *Cyprus Tigers* (1990), you play a henchman very well. It's kind of a silly question, but I was curious what you thought made a good henchman?

Sophia: Thank you, I enjoyed that role. I like silent henchmen. It's all in the eyes, right? I don't like villains that give long speeches right before they are about pop someone off. I like villains that are unpredictable and dangerous.

Chris: Tell me your thoughts on your last sequence in *Cyprus Tigers*. It has the big build-up where you're very menacingly walking in front of the car, and then there's a short but well-done fight scene with Simon Yam. I'm curious what your thoughts are on the build-up being longer than the fight scene.

Sophia: We simply ran out of time. They spent so long on the buildup that when we finally got into the garage there was no more time left for a big fight. Many of the locations were not paid for. I don't know if this one was or not. Most of the time they didn't have permits and some of the locations where we shot were run by Triads. There were no unions to protect you, so you had to look out for yourself. They shot quickly with very little set-up time. It was really a rag and bones production. I think that's why many of the movies during this time were so creative. There weren't a lot of producers or heads of studios coming down saying, "You can't do this. You must do that." Everybody had a free-for-all and did what they wanted. Sometimes it would work and sometimes it wouldn't.

The fight in the garage was fun. Simon was great to work with. I had a laugh falling on top of him. He is a really good sport. After spending so much time shooting Simon and Joey Wong, we only had a few hours left to shoot my fight. This was a just one of those little fights and then that's it. I did many of those!

Chris: You mention no unions. Did you ever have difficulty getting paid?

Sophia: Yes. There's one movie that I refused to go to set because we were almost at the end of shooting and I hadn't been paid yet. I said, "Look guys, you've got to give me something before we finish because I know you're going to run." I was very naïve and gullible when I first arrived in Hong Kong and many people took advantage of that. As the years went by, I started to wise-up and understand the system. I realized that if I wanted to get paid, I had to get it before we wrapped. The final year I was there, I went under contract with Yukari's company. She negotiated everything for me and got me a fairly large salary. In the very beginning, I would work for almost nothing, and I could hardly afford to eat. I lacked experience. Later, it was so helpful having someone backing me up, protecting and promoting me.

In the beginning, I was always paid in cash. I would look around set and find the guy who was supposed to be paying people. He would pull out a roll of cash from his pocket and pay me. There were never any checks. I don't know where the money was coming from, and I never asked.

Chris: There's a movie you broke your foot in.

Sophia: *Story of the Gun* (1992; aka *Lethal Girls 2* and *Guns of the Master Killer*). That's the fight on the boat. They shot my character in the leg to cover it. I broke my foot during the fight scene in the building, though. It was a stupid thing because it was a tiny gag. Being an inexperienced stunt performer, at the time, I didn't clear the area. All I had to do was jump through a hole in the wall. When I landed my foot rolled over a rock, and I snapped a bone. That's the first time I snapped any bone, so I kept going. In a scene with Gordon

Lui, I ran down the hill with the broken foot, but I didn't realize it. My foot was so swollen up. After shooting that day, I took myself to the hospital. I went in and the doctor laughed at me because I said, "I think I've broken my foot." He said, "Yeah, sure you have." He took an Xray and then came out, waving his hand as I started hobbling towards him. He yelled, "No! Don't move. You broke your foot!" He put a cast on my foot, but we couldn't finish the movie without shooting that big end sequence with Yukari and me on the boat. The director said, "Look, we have to shoot the end fight scene. I desperately need you for that sequence. Please, will you do it?" I cut the cast off my foot myself and bandaged it tightly. I said, "I'll do the best I can. Let's do it."

Chris: In both *Cyprus Tigers* and *Story of the Gun* you get shot in the leg but continue to fight. It reminded me of the famous Bruce Lee versus Chuck Norris fight scene where Chuck continues to fight despite being severely injured. Do you feel the injuries helped the fight scenes?

Sophia: Maybe it did, but this was real and it was very painful. We were filming the fight scene in a boat on choppy water with waves hitting the sides. It was very tricky trying to balance on one leg and fight. I could barely stand up. However, I was pleased with how it came out. It was worth the effort, and the director had a smile on his face when I flipped backwards off the boat into the water. Scene done!

Chris: *Angel Terminators 2* (1991) has another great fight scene at the end. Take me from how you were approached for the role to training, including the machine gun and fight scene.

Sophia: I can't remember how I got that job; I think someone just paged me. I was beginning to do more wire-gags, and I did my first one to my stomach. I think I experienced my first explosion on this and firing the machine gun was great fun. My fights were getting longer, but I still didn't have any agent or anybody doing deals for me. I would just take my headshot from studio to studio and beg personally. I had fun on this movie, and I enjoyed this round with Moon.

At the time of doing this movie, I felt like I was becoming a part of the Yukari and Moon team. It felt good fighting with them now because the first couple of years I felt so awkward and uncomfortable doing any fights. For me, it was one, two, three and duck. By the time I got to do *Angel Terminators 2*, I didn't have to think so much about what I was doing, and I could be in the scene and in the moment more. I didn't have to worry about how I was holding my hands or whatever. I was just starting to make progress, so that was the beginning of a better time for me. The first years were a struggle because certain people had expectations of me. For me to try and meet those expectations at the time was huge pressure and very frustrating. I didn't ever want to disappoint anybody. I wanted to be good. By the time I got to do *Angel Terminators 2*, I felt like, "Now I can fight with you a bit." It was a great feeling. Moon and I got on really well during that shoot.

Chris: What are your thoughts on the "Girls with Guns" movement?

Sophia: I wish it could have gone on forever. Honestly, I think I would have been happy doing that for twenty years. I'm not searching for fame anymore, but I do love fighting. I really enjoyed the creativity in those films, and it was a time when they let the girls loose. They let the girls hit hard. They let the girls take hard reactions and hit the ground. They let the girls look fierce. I just loved that they gave women strength and empowerment. I'm really grateful to have been a very small part of it.

Chris: In *Sword of Honor*, your character has to prove her worth before being a part of the action. What are some examples in your career where you had to prove yourself when you shouldn't have needed to?

Sophia: A lot of times I have had to prove myself simply because I am in a tough business. You say you can do a stunt, but then you have to do it. Talk is cheap. Stunt work is a competitive industry. Whether you are training in the gym or you are performing on set, you are constantly challenging your skills and proving yourself to the people around you. The pressure to perform perfectly each take can be intense, and you would hope that you wouldn't need to prove yourself after so many years, yet it never really goes away. It keeps you on your toes.

Chris: *Sword of Honor* **was a disappointment for me because your character has a couple of fight scenes outside the car and in the training facility but she ends up in the hospital. I was expecting her to kick ass in the second half.**

Sophia: Yes, not much of a battle for me. Not all American producers are big fans of Hong Kong films. This wasn't my movie. It was a Steven Leigh movie, and my name only appeared later as a star after people realized that there was a cult following with me. The movie was for Steven and all about building him as a lead. I could have been played by anybody. There was no special interest in building my character. So, yeah, this movie was a disappointment for me also.

Chris: Tell me your thoughts on your role in the following films: *China Heat* **(1992).**

Sophia: I hurt my back jumping over the rail on this movie. It really affected my fight because I couldn't twist my body and kicking was difficult. I was wearing a windbreaker in the jump, and it was extremely windy in Shanghai. The windbreaker covered my face, so I couldn't spot my landing. I landed on my stomach and really hurt my spine. The stunt person inside of me decided to not tell anyone and keep going. I couldn't move very well, so I was disappointed in my performance. Isabelle was a little tough to work with. She always was. I only did a few days on that shoot. The rest of the time I went and explored Shanghai. That was great.

Chris: *The Big Deal* **(1992).**

Sophia: I loved it. Everything in Hong Kong was over the top, whether you were fighting or acting. I got to play a character who could be wild. It was meant to be fun. It was a goofy comedy. Everybody was in such good spirits when they were working on it. There was a lot of laughter on set. I didn't feel any of the racist tension that I felt on other sets. My salary had gone up, so maybe people respected me more and treated me better. The whole scene in the playground took a long time to film. We went back and forth, back and forth. It was the first time I got to do comedy. I really loved just being an idiot.

Chris: *U.S. Seals 2*.

Sophia: Right before I shot *U.S Seals 2*, I did the Buffy video game and sprained my foot. Then one week before I left, I herniated two lower disks. I was on my back, thinking what the hell was I doing going to Bulgaria? I hadn't had the opportunity to play a part in a movie in a while, and I was determined to go regardless. I put ice on my back and numbed the pain with pills and just got on with it. I was working with a solid group of people, all martial artists. I could throw a kick, and they could take it. I love people who aren't afraid of taking a hit, and I don't want them to be afraid to hit me. In the past, I have fought with certain guys that say, "I'm not fighting you. I never hit a woman." Why am I in a fight scene with a guy if he just wants to bitch slap me without me doing anything? A long time ago, I was shooting a movie, and I wanted to do a Hong Kong spin as a reaction to a hit I was getting. The guy said, "Women don't do that. You can't do that. That's not what a woman would do." All the guys were doing it. What's the difference?

Chris: How involved was Isaac in the fight scenes for *U.S. Seals 2*?

Sophia: Isaac didn't do any of my fights, but he did some of the others. Andy Cheng did mine. Isaac directed me in my acting portions only. Isaac is a funny guy. I liked working with him.

Chris: What do you think shows your best work?

Sophia: *Buffy* would be the closest.

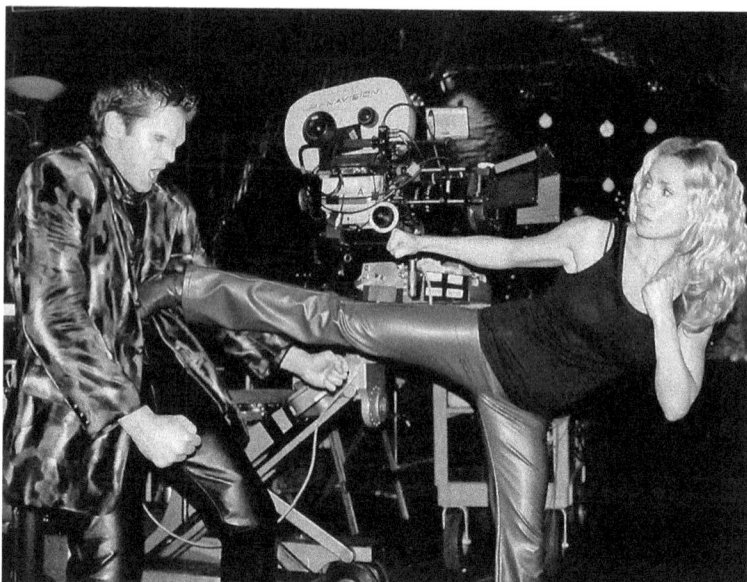

Sophia Crawford on the set of *Buffy the Vampire Slayer.*
Photo courtesy of Sophia Crawford.

Chris: We will talk about your stunt work later since it's your main line of work now, but do you still audition?

Sophia: No, I don't have an agent. I haven't had one in years. When I did *Mighty Morphin Power Rangers* and *Buffy*, I was so busy with stunts that the agent I had in the beginning dropped me like a lead weight. Once my stunt career took off, it was like a double-edged sword because I realized I was being seen as a stuntwoman and not as an actress. It was different from being in Hong Kong where actors were martial artists also. When I added stunts to my resume, auditions were hard to come by. I think nowadays things have progressed. Stunt people are given many more opportunities to do acting roles like never before. Thankfully, things have changed a bit.

Chris: Was there any other point where you were pitched as a possible lead for a film?

Photo courtesy of Sophia Crawford.

Sophia: I haven't had that many opportunities. Isaac wrote that part for me in *U.S Seals 2*, and Jeff wrote a script for me years ago called *Nexus*. It got close to being shot but eventually got shelved.

Chris: Does that disappoint you?

Sophia: Sure, it does a little bit. I sometimes wonder if I had come along a few years later, maybe things would have been different. I seemed to have been ahead of my time. But then I would have missed the "Girls with Guns" era, so maybe it just wasn't meant to be. After the success of shows like *Buffy*, *Xena*, and *Alias*, roles improved significantly for women doing action. Then there was the huge success of *The Matrix* (1999) and women suddenly became front and

31

center, fighting with the guys. When I came to Los Angeles, you didn't really get a chance to do much of a fight. It was always about the guys. At one time, I was pushing to be a female lead action star, but there weren't that many opportunities. Then, I got into stunts and became very busy. I just focused on stunts. I loved it, and a little piece of me inside gave up on acting. I felt like I wasn't going to have any success at it. I felt I could have success in stunts, and I was achieving it. These days, people's perception of girls fighting tough is completely different. Despite my disappointments, I really don't have many complaints. Nonetheless, I've had a brilliant time. I've really loved it.

Chris: What difficulties have you faced as a stuntwoman?

Sophia: Being a stuntwoman is much different from being an actor. The difficulties as a stuntwoman are about maintaining your physical skills and maintaining your health, especially on a show like *Buffy*. I had to fight continuously for nine months non-stop. It was so hard on the body. Bruise after bruise after sprain. It's a challenging job, and it is still a male-dominated business. There are a lot of politics involved. Working as a stunt person is a submissive role. You have to work through the coordinator, and everything is channeled through them. You have a lot of responsibility in your performance as a stunt person. As an actor, you fuck it up, you do another take, and nobody cares because you're the actor. If you're a stunt person and you mess up, your career could be done. There's no room for error as a stunt person. You could get killed or kill someone else. If you keep failing on a stunt, nobody's going to hire you again. The challenge is with yourself and all in the performance of your action. It's not how you deliver a line, although these days it's a bonus if you can act too. It's more to do with how you are received as a person, how hard you train, and how you work together as a team. It's a different mentality. I gravitated more toward that because I don't have to be showered with, "You're a star," and those diva things. I don't have to be the star.

I'm happy just being a part of filmmaking. I don't care whose face is on screen. I only care about good fight, a good script, and good entertainment.

Chris: What do you consider to be your most difficult stunt to date?

Sophia: There were a few that were tough. One of the difficult ones was on *G.I. Joe* (2009) when we did a multi-level high fall. It was a tandem fall, meaning you're entwined with another person. The first level had a box that was only three feet wide, which was rather small. The second level was bigger. The way they edited it though, we could've shot it in pieces. We did it in one. What made it challenging is that we were on a lift that was moving up. The platform that we were standing on was rising as we were fighting, and then we had to find our mark at the edge of the platform and the three-foot box. All those elements made it challenging and the stunt really tricky. Another one that I found a little bit scary was one time when I jumped from a helicopter on to a moving train. It wasn't a high jump, but I hate flying. I had never been in a helicopter, and then I'm circling a train with the other people being told, "Jump! Jump!" My heart was in my throat, but it was easy. Why did I get so excited and anxious over it? After I did it, I was like, "It was great!" Sometimes, prior to a stunt you will get that rush, but that's the time when you bring your focus to your center, and you try to calm your breathing. You calm yourself so you can focus. You can't focus when you've got all this stuff going on in your head. People don't realize that in stunts we're not just thinking about the fight, but we have a peripheral view of the camera. We have to keep that view every time we kick, punch, or do a reaction to make sure it's a hit. Then we have to hit the marks on the ground and sell it hard. It's definitely a technical and physical job. You have to learn about rigging, equipment, ratchets, and many different things that aren't just fighting. It's always challenging no matter what you're doing in stunts. It could be a very small thing, but you're doing it in seven-inch heels or you've got a mask on and can't see. Now what was an easy stunt is damn near impossible. That's where you go, "Focus. Get it done right and be safe."

Chris: Other interviewees have spoken about stunt work being dominated by men. Would you agree and how have you dealt with this?

Sophia: It's true. The stunt business is still dominated by men, but there are plenty of excellent stuntwomen out there too. There are some great female fighters out there now. The way I have dealt with this whole male domination thing is the same way I have dealt with similar situations in the past: I don't give a damn.

Chris: There are other women with similar backgrounds as you who do stunt work. I'm thinking of Bridgett "Baby Doll" Riley and Diana Lee Inosanto who do stunt work with a martial arts background.

Sophia: A martial arts background definitely helps for sure. I have worked for more than two decades using my martial arts as a specialty, but you do need to acquire other skills too. You rarely have longevity in stunts if all you can do is fight. It is very important to learn a variety of stunt skills. Both Bridgett and Diana have been very successful in the film industry because of their legitimate fighting and stunt skills.

Chris: Who do you consider to be a Bad Ass Woman of Cinema?

Sophia: My idol, Yukari Oshima.

DIANA LEE
INOSANTO

Diana Lee Inosanto is a member of martial arts royalty who has created a career for herself. Her father is martial arts legend Dan Inosanto. Diana grew up surrounded by martial arts, including her godfather, Bruce Lee. Training in martial arts may have been expected, but, at that time, she was a female going into a male-dominated field. Diana would perform in theaters, including East West Players and the Lodestone Theater Ensemble. Stuntwork makes up the majority of Diana's filmography: she did stunts for movies such as *Blade* (1998), *The Patriot* (2000), and *Face/Off* (1997), along with the television shows *Walker, Texas Ranger* and *Buffy the Vampire Slayer*. In addition to stunts, she took supporting roles in the films *The Vault* (2005) and *The Prodigy* (2005) before embarking on producing. Diana produced, wrote, directed,

Photo courtesy of Diana Lee Inosanto.

and starred in *The Sensei* (2008). The film revolves around a woman with a black belt teaching a bullied, gay teenager. The controversial subject matter created an uphill production battle, but the finished product proved worth the fight. *The Sensei* has played at numerous festivals, winning awards and applause. The film has also proven socially important, becoming a tool in the fight against bullying. Diana Lee Inosanto is as much a skilled filmmaker and stuntwoman as martial artist.

<u>Notable roles</u>
The Sensei
Buffy the Vampire Slayer

Chris: How would you describe your childhood?

Diana: It was very colorful. I realize, looking back with my adult eyes, it was definitely very unique. When you have Danny Inosanto as your father and Bruce Lee as your godfather, you're bound to have a different childhood and perspective on life. Overall, I thought my childhood was great. I was very lucky because I grew up around the who's who of the martial arts world. Although, at the time, I didn't know they were the who's who of the martial arts world; I just thought they were a bunch of unique people who loved to hit, kick, sweat, and punch each other. They were awesome with me. It was a great way for me to explore what it is to be in an all-male environment. I was pretty much raised with male energy my whole life. It probably prepared me as a woman to work in male dominated fields as an adult.

Chris: At what age did you begin practicing martial arts?

Diana: I started training in martial arts from the time I was a toddler, but it wasn't in a formal sense. My father made it like play. He made it very game-like. As a child, I had no idea I was being trained. I just knew I was having fun playing with dad as soon as I could walk. When I got a little older, it became more formalized. My father would sometimes throw me in the class. It would be all these big, huge men. I didn't care. I was having fun. It became formalized at the age of six or seven. I had an encounter with a group of girls who were bullying me. They tried scratching out my face. I started to take self-defense very seriously.

Chris: What advice would you give a woman considering pursuing martial arts?

Diana: First, you need to find a school where you feel comfortable, and then interview the instructor. Make sure they are connected to your needs. I've heard of schools absolutely terrifying women and chasing them away as they don't feel safe. Start with doing research and homework. Talk with the administrators of the school you're considering, and see how sensitive they are to you being a woman. Luckily, we live in the digital age so you can find out a lot about the school and its reputation.

If I knew nothing about martial arts I would start with Thai boxing, which is a quick art to learn. It's aggressive, and gets you in shape quickly. I think it's very effective on the streets. It's not necessarily considered a pretty art, like what you see in kung fu movies, but it's resourceful. Thai boxing involves head butts and knees. From a self-defense view, I think it carries exactly what women need to protect themselves on the street. Also, learn some form of Filipino martial arts—something like knife self-defense. It's important to learn how to defend yourself and disarm a weapon. Then, of course, there's learning how to deal with the ground. There are a lot of rape prevention groups that throw you on the ground, and you learn how to kick off an assailant. Jujitsu might be good for that.

Chris: What have you learned from your father?

Diana: I'm thankful that my dad gave me the gift of martial arts. At times I was reluctant and wanted to do other things like play with my Barbie dolls. In hindsight, this was his gift to me. It prepared me for life, particularly by being raised around male energy and interacting with so many different men from unusual walks of life. It helped prepare me for my life as a stuntwoman, working in the martial arts industry, and working as a filmmaker running a crew of predominantly males. It's almost like the book *Men Are From Mars, Women Are From Venus*. Men are wired in a different way. I thank my father for giving me that insight. The other thing my dad taught me is compassion. He taught me about being sensitive and patient. These are all traits that my dad really emphasized. He taught me how to look at things in a different perspective. If I get angry, he taught me how to take a step back. I try to see it from the other person's angle and where they may be coming from. He encouraged a balance in mind, body and spirit.

Chris: You obtained a degree in literature. Did you have ideas for another direction in your career?

Diana: It was really tough because I wanted to try finishing up my bachelor's in literature and maybe one day go to law school. My problem is that I got married very young in life, and I had an autistic son. When you are the parent of a developmentally disabled child, you don't have the kind of luxuries that other people have, such as not being able to go to a movie with your child. It's a different road, and I was a single mother for a while too. It was very hard on me. At one point I decided to shift gears, and I was thinking of being a policewoman. It was shortly after the L.A. riots, but they were trying to recruit more women. I had signed up and began taking the initial test. The timing was weird because I also ended up finding work at 20th Century Fox where I was actually working in human resources. Finally, I became interested in being a stuntwoman because of my martial arts ability, since I knew how to fight and do different forms of martial arts. It's kind of strange how that all happened.

Chris: It's interesting that you're at least the third interviewee who considered or pursued being a policewoman.

Diana: Particularly in Los Angeles, they had done some studies that women were able to, for whatever reason, calm domestic disputes much faster than men. I was definitely considering it.

Chris: What was the deciding factor to go into film?

Diana: I always wanted to go into film. During my early days of being a stuntwoman, I'd always thought it was fascinating. There's no doubt the men were calling the shots, and they had a lot of power to persuade what kind of projects were being made. I wasn't blind to that, even in my early days. Also, I was a struggling actress. I started to see that the power was in being a filmmaker. I thought, "Gosh, there aren't any female directors." When looking at the history of the Oscars, there had never been a woman who had won. My mother had reminded me that when my godfather was pursuing his career in Hollywood and was rejected for doing kung fu, he was really falling under hard financial times. Bruce Lee contemplated going to Hong Kong to maybe jumpstart his career over there. He was really clear to my parents that he was the captain of his own ship and could design his own destiny. He makes circumstances. She reminded me of that and, eventually, I really started watching the directors and producers on the sets where I worked. There were a lot of A-list projects, and I started asking questions. I started taking workshops with Doug Simms, while preparing myself to take this journey and be a filmmaker.

Chris: Were you on set with your father before you started doing stuntwork?

Diana: I was a little girl. I remember going to San Francisco and being on the set of *Killer Elite* (1975), which was directed by Sam Peckinpah and starred James Caan. I was amazed by the process of this set and all of these people coming together. Then, my father had worked on a television project, which was a *C.H.I.P.S.* spinoff. I loved the process.

Chris: Were you ever concerned about the challenges you might face in either martial arts or film because you are a female?

Photo courtesy of Diana Lee Inosanto.

Diana: Sure, martial arts are a different challenge. When you come from a
family like mine, I've been told it's like being considered martial arts
royalty. That may sound fun and glamorous, but, on the other hand,
it can be difficult. You'll have people who will stalk you and then

people who might be sort of crazy and challenge you. They project whatever they want to project on you because maybe they feel they can conquer, challenge, or beat you up. They think that will build them and their reputation up. The politics is one thing I didn't like about the martial arts world. My father was graceful when he dealt with the politics and tried to never judge somebody. He wouldn't be quick to speak out on somebody even when I felt he had every right to. People would say horrible things about him, but he would take the high road and appeal to his higher angels and kept focusing on his teaching. That's the best thing you can do.

It was very clear to me, even now, how difficult the road is for women filmmakers. Women only put out seven percent of the projects in Hollywood. That's a horrible, horrible number. Hollywood is not liberal like people want to think. There's room for great improvement. I'm not afraid to throw my hat in the ring and do what I've got to do to make it.

Chris: You mentioned the people challenging you. Can you speak about an experience you've had?

Diana: The majority of people I've met at seminars and martial arts events have been very respectful. However, one time I was at an event and this one guy, a young blood, countered me at a seminar that my husband and I were teaching. We were explicitly working on a different kind of technique. Just to be a jerk, he countered me to prove something. I remember thinking, "If I do what I normally would do on the streets, he could turn around and sue me." We're living in a modern age and that's one of the things that a martial arts teacher needs to be cautious about. If I have one of these students who decide to challenge me and I counter him, he may turn around and try to sue. That sort of thing hangs over the head of a martial artist. At the time, I didn't do anything to him because I realized it was a professional setting. After that incident, I talked to an attorney. Now when I teach seminars, I make sure I do a step process saying,

"May I touch you? May I show you this?" I hate to do that, but it's to protect me legally so that if I do have some guy that comes at me I'm going to do what I do on the streets. I can say, "I asked him and he decided to do something else." I've also had certain situations like when I was at my dad's academy and ended up sparring this guy who was visiting from Europe. He didn't know who I was at the time, and I didn't know him beyond being a visiting student. For whatever reason, he decided to go hard on me. My father was telling us to spar at fifty percent. The student was going hard, and my husband was watching from a distance going, "Wow, this guy is out of control." It's rough when you're a woman because sometimes certain men will look at that and go, "I have to make sure and put her in her place. She can't look good, or I'll look bad." I remember I had to just go after him. Men have been known to go through this too. That's something I don't like about the martial arts world.

Chris: Did you feel you had to work harder because you were a female?

Diana: Yes, absolutely. Physically and diplomatically I had to work harder to not react but respond. Being an Inosanto or Bruce Lee's goddaughter, I had to really try to be wise, diplomatic, listen to people, and couldn't be quick to anger. People may say something negative. They have a right to an opinion, and it's none of my business what people think. What matters most is my family. I conduct myself to the best ability possible and try to be a good human being.

Chris: What inspired you to create the story of *The Sensei*?

Diana: I'm glad you asked that question. There were several moments in my life that collectively inspired *The Sensei*. I grew up around a wonderful man named Gil Johnson, who actually was the coeditor of *Tao of Jeet Kune Do*, which is still the leading martial arts book in the world. He was a very close family friend, not only to the Lees but also the Inosantos. He helped my father on his book. Gil was one of my favorite adults and a straight man who used to work for *Black Belt Magazine*. From time to time, he would have his own column.

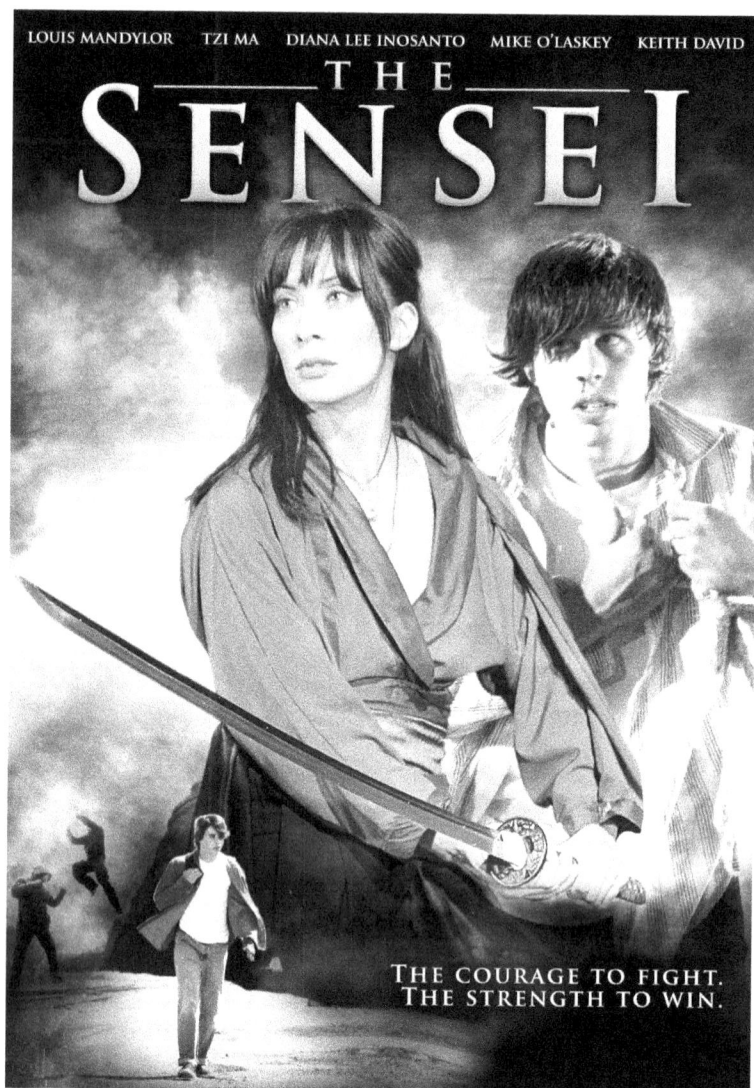

Poster for *The Sensei.* Photo courtesy of Diana Lee Inosanto.

He had traveled to Northern Africa and returned. The next thing we know, we see him on television and he was an advocate for what was happening with the AIDS epidemic. That's how we learned Gilbert had AIDS, contracting it from a blood transfusion. You have to remember the timing of the AIDS epidemic era. Everyone kept saying in America that it was a gay disease. Because we knew Gilbert, I learned really quickly as a teenager that this is not just a disease but an illness that can impact anyone. If we're not careful it's going to grow, and sure enough it did. I never forgot his role modeling and the example he lead. He was such a wonderful, dignified man. Despite what the culture and all the people who were homophobic wanted to project, he held his head high and did it with dignity. He is one of my heroes. You had to flash forward to the 1990s and the Matthew Shepherd murders. If you don't remember who he was, he's the young man who was kidnapped, beaten, tortured, and left tied to a post. It became a landmark case because it brought to light the issue of discrimination and hatred toward gays. At that time my cousin was coming out as a gay woman, and I started connecting with what Gilbert was going through. What would have happened if Matthew had learned martial arts or trained heavy? Would he have had a chance? Those were the beginning seeds in making *The Sensei*.

Chris: After you wrote the script, did you know you were going to direct the film?

Diana: No, I didn't know I was going to direct it. In my heart, I wanted to. I knew I was going to have the task of trying to be in it in the way Melvin Van Peebles did. I saw him speak, and I knew out of the gate that it was going to have a tiny budget. To find an actress who can do both martial arts, act, and be flexible with a tiny budget wasn't going to happen. It was then that I knew I would have to play the lead. While searching to find a director, I knew I wanted this to be a very poignant, serious film. It takes issues very seriously. There's bullying of a gay teenage boy. For some reason, all the directors wanted to do it like this cheap kind of B-martial-arts- movie. I was like, "No, you're losing the point. This is supposed to be a movie that can easily go into Sundance." It's not supposed to be some B-film where we slop together a bunch of fight scenes and carry on. It should be delivered with some sensitivity. As I talked to a writer, he emphasized, "You know, Diana, with your background I think you can direct. You have an acting background. You have a stage background. You have a lot of theater behind you. You've been on a lot of sets. You can do this." It was then I decided I was going to be the guardian and protector of this script. My goal was to multi-task, and I set out to be an Edward Burns or even my godfather where he played many roles on a set. It was scary, but I did it. I discovered I love directing.

Chris: Do you feel by producing and directing you were empowered?

Diana: Absolutely. I have to say, there was something amazing about that too. I could say, "I am a director. I am a producer." There was a sense of empowerment that came with that. It's interesting how people look at you differently. They react to you inversely. It's amazing for me. While attending the Raindance film festival in London, this guy assumed I was just an actress and he goes, "I'm the director, I'm this…" I was able to go, "Oh, interesting. I'm a director too." The shift and dichotomy of that conversation just shifted because now I was an equal with him. I wanted to be able to have a dialogue about directing and making movies and producing. It has happened a few times.

Chris: What did you draw from as your character faces prejudice as a female in *The Sensei*?

Diana: I am very aware in my travels as a martial artist teacher that there are systems and, unfortunately, styles that do not give women their instructorships. For whatever reason, they feel like they can't carry on the system. Some of that might be cultural, and some of that might be a deep-seated belief that martial arts is a man's place. It bothers me seeing this. Particularly, being Dan Inosanto's daughter, if you go to my father's academy you'll see his influences. He's not shy about showing the diverse style and systems he's studied. I was very aware that the instructors and Masters within some of those styles really had an issue with women. How sad and unfortunate. I was able to throw that into my screenplay. I wanted very much to really focus on the nature of prejudice. That's what *The Sensei* was about and how we deal with the various levels of it, from extreme to very subtle.

Chris: Did you face any opposition to the gay theme?

Diana: In the beginning, there were people who were uncomfortable. I think they would rather have me do a low-budget version of *Karate Kid* (1984), but I really wanted to address this issue about tolerance and bullying. Even when my movie came out, I had some threats, and that was very difficult. People who wouldn't identify themselves were threatening people who would cover me PR wise. They were making threats to my cast and my crew. The level of hatred really bothered me. I felt very strongly about this. I, for one, know how to deal with prejudice being a bi-racial woman, having a white mother and an Asian father. They were married in a time when most of the country had a ban on interracial marriage. California was one of the few states that allowed for interracial marriage. Still, nationwide, the ban on interracial marriage wasn't lifted until something like 1968. Even when the ban was lifted, I saw firsthand what our family had to go through. It was not easy. I didn't know what the words racism or discrimination meant. I could feel this energy when we would walk into a restaurant. It was very difficult. The only place I felt safe was in our martial arts circles. When I wrote *The Sensei*, dealing with what was happening in the gay community, I absolutely connected to their pain and political frustrations, resonating with and understanding that. How could I, as a martial artist and somebody that tries to be a spiritual woman, turn a blind eye to that? Our film actually ended up getting a lot of attention because we were in the Associated Press. One of the schools where we had tried filming belonged to the same school district as Columbine. They turned us down, and I couldn't find a high school that would accept us in the metropolitan area of Denver. As frustrating as it was to go through, it was also amazing that we got the press we did for trying to make this movie.

Chris: Tell me about your experience on *The Prodigy* and, in particular, your fight scene.

Diana: It depends on who it was under the costume. Sometimes it was my husband, sometimes it was just different people in the crew chasing me up and down the stairs. *The Prodigy* was just a straight role for me as an actress, but I was also Associate Producer on that. It gave me a break from being these warrior women characters. I loved working on *The Prodigy* and with Will Kaufman, who was the director. A lot of their crew members worked on *The Sensei*. My husband did an amazing job of choreographing some of the fight scenes and received a great write up in the *Daily Variety*. It was a great project to work on. I have to admit it was amazing to be running up the stairs while having a man run after me with a knife. To run away from him when I've been taught to disarm was kind of funny. It was my job to be a victim.

Chris: Did you ever feel that your fight scenes were gratuitous in *The Vault*?

Diana: I did not produce or direct *The Vault*. Honestly, I was not pleased with *The Vault*. It probably pushed me more to be a director. I had some say on some of the fights but no say on the editing. When you're an actor, you're very vulnerable. If the editors, directors, or producers aren't doing their job, an actor may not look that great onscreen. I'm just a player. I'm a piece on the chess board. The one thing that was evident to me when I did *The Vault* was, again, how vulnerable an actor is. You could have an amazing actor, but if people aren't on their game as far as directing and editing, you can look like an amateur. It's really horrible.

Chris: You do a lot of acting that borders more dramatic than your typical action star. I had a meeting once with Richard Norton. It was interesting because I had a background in horror films, and I was trying to get into action films. Richard had the background in

action films and was trying to get away from that. Do you have that desire to avoid being typecast in a particular genre?

Diana: Oh yeah. I was a producer on *Sinners and Saints* (2010). It's completely different than *The Sensei*. It's a pure action film. It's like an edgy *Lethal Weapon* (1987). I'm very proud of it. Both my husband and I were producers on it. I did the action design for the Los Angeles unit and part of the Dallas unit. My husband focused on Louisiana and Dallas with me. I want color in my career. I really want a colorful palette in which to make films and projects. I do have sort of a horror project I'm trying to develop right now. Also, there's a musical I'm trying to get off the ground. I don't mind doing action projects, but I'd rather it be something in the vein of *The Hurt Locker* (2008). One of my biggest dreams is to do a movie on the Navy Seal. I grew up around Navy Seals because of my father. So, I definitely want to expand my horizons.

Chris: Why have, or would, you turn down a role?

Diana: Script or maybe nudity. I'm not keen on nudity unless it's something like *Schindler's List* (1993) or something for artistic reasons. I like scripts to be either fun, put together well, or I know the director is capable.

Chris: Have you ever had to use your martial arts skills outside of work?

Diana: All the time. Not in the way that people would traditionally think. If you are talking physically, yeah, there have been very light moments. True martial arts to me prepare you to prevent conflict. It teaches you to be aware of your environment. I have been in certain circumstances with girlfriends. We would have a gang of guys around us, and I basically had to pretend I had a weapon in my jacket. My girlfriend was also a kickboxer. We put our girlfriends between us and made it clear we weren't victims and would be ready. Then they left us alone. It was a real standoff—it was bizarre. There have been moments where I'm in a bar and some drunken guy tries to grab on to me, and I side-sweep him. Things like that. Honestly where I feel my martial arts have played a daily influence is in my daily interactions with people when I try to focus, stay relaxed, and do the best job possible. That's all you can do. The majority of people who learn martial arts will never have to deal with an encounter.

Chris: What do you consider to be your most difficult stunt?

Diana: The scariest one for me was in the pilot for *Buffy the Vampire Slayer* because I had a previous injury that didn't allow me to operate at 100 percent. I had gotten a call from a stunt coordinator who was helping out another friend. He said, "Hey, they're looking for a double, and you look like you are the same size as Sarah Michelle Gellar." I went in and met with the stunt coordinator and the director Joss Whedon. They chose me. In one day, they had us doing all these stunts. We were crashing into boxes. A bulldog was my first assignment. It's all about the presentation, and part of it was never even shown on TV. It was some hairy stuff. I was already injured from Thai boxing. There's nothing worse than trying to do a stunt and you're already injured. Because I grew up around my dad and Jeff Imada, I've always been cautious about safety. The only scary stunt I've been on was a non-union music video. I didn't like being there. They were setting off explosions. This is before music videos were a part of SAG. My thought was, "This is not good." There was no communication with the stunt coordinators. We were on top of where they put airplanes in Van Nuys. We were 150 feet in the air, and they were setting off explosions beneath us. The roof had tiles that were loose. I just thought, "This is ridiculous." I tend to want to know who the people I'm working with are. Everyone else I've worked with has been great, responsible stunt people. I've been very blessed. I've work with the best in the stunt world.

Chris: What are some of the injuries you've attained from stuntwork?

Diana: I have lower back problems. I'm sure that's a little bit with the martial arts too. Back problems, shoulder injuries, and maybe some knee injuries. I've been very fortunate. I haven't had to do some of the hairy stuff like my stunt sisters have. I know high falls are not my forte so I stay away from it. I did driving stunts in John Woo's movie *Face/Off*. That was really fun. The stunt culture in Hollywood is so unique, diverse, and awe-inspiring. There are some great memories. While I fight for the next project, I'm hoping to do a movie about the stuntworld.

Chris: What do you see as the largest misconception about stuntwork?

Diana: That you can pull in just anybody to do a stunt. Most of the true stunt people specialize in a certain area, but there are people who think it's an easy thing. I see this with producers and directors. One thing I don't like about film school is that one dynamic they miss is teaching about safety. I hate that. Sometimes, no matter how safe you try to make it, there will still be problems and accidents that happen. It's a very dangerous job. I watched this documentary that said stuntwork is considered one of the top ten dangerous jobs in the world. Even more dangerous than being a police officer because you never know when certain elements of a set will go wrong. You just never know. It is important to be on your guard all the time. Of course, if you're working super long hours and a production is trying to cut corners, then it can get really dangerous. I think the hard part with stunts is when you have to work with another team from another country. Other countries have their own sensibilities about stunts. I love Hong Kong cinema, but I'm clearly aware the stunt community in Hong Kong takes way more risks that you would never take in America. That's why Hong Kong movies have a lot more injuries and stuntmen who have died or been permanently maimed. Here, in America, especially for insurance purposes, you really work hard to make sure the safety of your actors and stuntpeople are set because you don't want to have something like what happened on the *Twilight Zone: The Movie* (1983) set or with Brandon on *The Crow* (1994).

Chris: What do you believe are the characteristics of a good stuntwoman?

Diana: The stuntworld is predominantly male-dominated, so you are going to have to deal. For a woman in the stunt field, she's going to have to learn to work with men. She's got to be professional. No crying on a set. I hate to say that, but you have to deal with it and possibly some pain. Stunt coordinators want to know that you are capable of handling the job and being professional. Also, the stunt coordinators are putting a lot of their trust in you to be safe. They have the producers and director looking at them to make sure they run the safety of the set in a smooth manner. I think for stuntwomen you have to stay in shape, know your field, and know when to say "No," to a stunt. That's really important. I've heard of stuntwomen where they were prepared to do one kind of stunt, but someone may ask for something different. Then the stuntwoman feels that because of pressure they have to say "Yes," to it, but I'm going "No." My philosophy is you have to be honest about where your comfort zone and your abilities are. Perhaps another suggestion can be offered.

Chris: What are your thoughts on the way women are depicted in martial arts?

Diana: Depending on what country. Here in the United States, there are certain cultures and styles that don't like women. They don't believe they can be a good guardian of the art. Then there are some instructors who are evolved. They are great. You see huge improvements with schools across the country. When I was a kid, I was one of maybe eight women in the country learning Filipino martial arts. Now you see this explosion of all these kids learning martial arts, and that's a good thing. With each passing generation, it's only going to get better. Some improvements could be made in Europe. I remember my first time in Paris: it was like 100 men and not one woman. I was going to teach with my husband. They were all aware that I was Danny Inosanto's daughter, but I just looked at these men, "Where are your girlfriends? Where are your wives? Why are they not here?" I thought it was peculiar, but the next time I came back to Paris they actually brought their girlfriends, sisters, or mothers. I was so pleased with that. It takes role modeling. When they saw I could move and work with my husband, they thought, "Wow, this is something that could be great for women in Europe."

Chris: What are some martial arts films that depict women in a way you appreciate?

Diana: I love *Crouching Tiger, Hidden Dragon* (2000). Ang Lee was one of my favorite directors before he even did that movie. Most people don't know he had a stage background. I love that movie and how the women were equals. They were vulnerable, yet share themselves emotionally with the men in that movie. It was amazing, and it's still my favorite martial arts film. He did that wonderfully.

Chris: Who do you consider to be a Bad Ass Woman of Cinema?

Diana: I still like Ripley in *Aliens* (1986). I know she doesn't do much martial arts, but I thought she was a bad ass woman. I love *Aliens*, and how James Cameron writes for women. I think *Terminator* (1984), the Sarah Connor with Linda Hamilton, is another example. I love how visceral and realistic they were. James Cameron is just an amazing director. He is one of my favorites because of how he writes for women. I liked what they were trying to do with Milla Jovovich in the *Resident Evil* films. My husband and I got to work Milla and train her for a while. That's kind of fun. I really think she pulled it off and did a great job. Of course, I love Michelle Yeoh. I loved her in *Supercop* (1992). I definitely have a soft spot for Michelle Yeoh, even before anyone in the United States knew who she was.

Laurene Landon as Hundra.
Photo courtesy of Laurene Landon.

LAURENE
LANDON

LAURENE LANDON HAS BEEN ACTING SINCE SHE WAS A CHILD. WHILE in the third grade, Landon performed in a play and found her love for acting in a foreshadowing role as a femme fatale. She would perform as an extra and model to make ends meet before landing her first major role in the wrestling film *All the Marbles* (1981), costarring Peter Falk. Landon's statuesque beauty, quick-witted personality, and athletic ability would lead to a duo of memorable sword and sandal films, *Hundra* (1983) and *Yellow Hair and the Fortress of Gold* (1984). Both films were directed by cult filmmaker Matt Cimber. Laurene filled out her career with a slew of films with another cult filmmaker, Larry Cohen, including the first two *Maniac Cop* movies. Laurene Landon's audience continues to build through revival screenings and rereleases, leading to multiple appearance opportunities around the world, including being a regular on the convention circuit. Laurene's impressive beauty, stunt work, and action prowess continue to garner her new fans.

<u>Notable roles</u>

Hundra

Maniac Cop

Yellow Hair and the Fortress of Gold

All the Marbles

Armed Response

Chris: Why did you decide to try and join the police academy?

Laurene: How did you know that? I didn't know that I ever told anybody about it. I wanted to be a policewoman because I just wanted to be a cop. I was an athlete, and I was very athletic all of my life. I wanted to be a police officer and can't explain why. It didn't last but sixteen weeks. I managed to do all the difficult, arduous training—the running and jogging and workouts they put you through. However, when it came time to go to the firing range I couldn't do it. I couldn't pull the trigger. I was too scared to shoot a clay duck. I realized I was too emotional to become a part of that occupation. If you can't shoot a clay duck then you certainly won't able to shoot a perp. The funny thing was, when I went to that class, the academy tried to weed people out. Initially there was something like a thousand people interviewing. There were probably fifteen women. I went in wearing a white polka-dot dress. It was summertime and very hot. I would wear the dress and high heels. I was a girly girl but a tomboy at the same time. They started weeding out all the weaklings. They pushed me around, calling me Betty Boop. That was my name for sixteen weeks. They tried to embarrass me, telling me my bra strap was showing. At one point, they wanted you to talk in front of a class about why you wanted to become a police officer. One of them yelled out, "Your bra strap is showing Betty Boop!" When they insulted the men, I noticed they would yell back. A lot of people quit at that moment. That's how they weeded people out initially. I thought it was all a joke. I didn't care. They're not going to make a fool out of me. I'll show them. I ended up quitting on myself. I was too emotional. You would think they would have figured that out before we were shooting. I had this attitude where I wanted to be a police officer.

Chris: How did you view the world of modeling?

Laurene: Boring. Stupid. It was only a quick way to make money. I could never sit still when I was being photographed. The photographers would look around for me, and I'd be climbing a tree or off somewhere else. I couldn't sit around, wait, and pose. I hated it. I only did it for the money.

Chris: How did you get the job on *All the Marbles*?

Laurene: I was up in Las Vegas for a pageant. They had narrowed it down to two or three women, and I was one of them. I was the only blonde. The other two were Spanish girls. While I was up there for this beauty pageant, I didn't get it. It went to a very beautiful, nice Spanish girl. I met a casting director in the same building. He said, "I'd love to cast you in a movie in Los Angeles. We're looking for very tall, beautiful women." He was telling me about the film and then said, "You look very athletic." I told him, "I am." He wrote down the number of a director I needed to see. I called and they said, "If Ruben says you're right then it means you're right for the interview." I went in and met all these people. I thought the director was Robert Altman, so I said to Robert Aldrich, "It's a pleasure meeting you Mr. Altman. I've heard a lot about you and your movies." He said, "Why did you call me Robert Altman?" I said, "That's your name." Everybody laughed and he said, "My name is Robert Aldrich." I said, "Who's that?" He thought it was ridiculously funny because they were all laughing. They said they were going to have a very vigorous auditioning process. They'd seen thousands of girls across the country. They're looking for wrestlers to train in acting. It didn't work, so they were looking for actors to train in wrestling. I had done some theater and some little budget movies like *Full Moon High* (1981). They were also looking for unknowns who had a little bit of experience. Paul Newman was going to do the movie at the time. I couldn't believe it and didn't think I had a chance. We auditioned and went through this process. All together, they had seen 2,000 girls. First, they auditioned us. I passed that, and I was sent to wrestling school to put us on videotape. Kathleen Turner and Peter Falk's wife were both going for the role. I thought Peter's wife was going to get it. We're wrestling off of White Oak in the Valley with these incredible, professional wrestlers. It was fun for me. It was athletic, and I loved it. I could do it easily. We had to do a lot of training. In the morning, we were running around baseball fields for an hour-and-a-half and doing leap frogs. We'd do all these activities and then the actor's strike hits. A lot of girls quit because it was against SAG rules. Vicky and I were the only ones who continued to wrestle. After the actor's strike was over, we just kept wrestling like nothing happened. We weren't getting paid at all, but that was fine. We were getting $800 a week before the strike, which to me was like $100,000. We went back after the strike, and they auditioned us again. They narrowed it down to twelve girls. Of the twelve, the studio executives and Robert looked at the screen tests. They said, "Out of the twelve of you, only four of you are going to wrestling school. If you want to quit, quit now because two of you are backups." All I needed to hear is that it's a competition. When I was in school, I was always competing for best athlete. A couple of the girls said they were going to quit. He reiterated repeatedly that only two were going to be in the movie. We all four stayed and, ultimately, they had us do choreographed stunts for studio heads. We did our routines individually with the trainers and were told to wait outside. In the meantime, one of the girls had broken her wrist, leaving only three of us. Robert Aldrich called in one girl, Judy Baldwin. She didn't come out. Apparently she went through another exit door in the office. Then they called me. He always called me Alf—someone running for President. Robert said, "You did a damned good job. You worked your ass off." He was staring out the window, and didn't say anything. I screamed, "You don't want me for your movie. I knew it. You don't want me for your movie. I'm no good." I started to cry and he says, "Sit down. No, you're playing the role of Molly." I said, "You want me in your movie? Why?" Everybody laughed. I didn't mean to be funny at all. I was terrified. I'm terrified talking about it now. I couldn't believe it, so I went out there to Vicky. He said, "Tell her it's bad news. She didn't get it. Don't let me down now!" I said, "You want me to say that to Vicky?" He said, "Yeah, tell her it's really bad for her." I went out and she asked me what happened. I said, "Everyone wants to see you inside. It doesn't look good. I'm so sorry Vicky, but it looks really bad." She stood up and walked by me expecting the worst. I heard her screaming inside, "Laurene!" She comes running out. I told her Robert wanted me to say that. That's how I got the part, but sorry it took four hours to tell you.

Chris: The movie depicted a lot of wild matches. Tell me about some of your experiences filming these.

Laurene: They were very difficult. In my opinion, the best wrestling moves we did were not used in the movie. We wrestled around three months of footage. Most of the wrestling footage was not used in the movie. Every day we would save the wrestling for after the dialogue was done. That was in case we got injured or broke a leg. Vicky or myself didn't make up the moves. The trainers made up all the moves. I can't take any credit for that whatsoever. They were so talented. I had no fear. My name was Fearless on set. I was so athletic that it was easy.

Chris: You got hurt, right?

Laurene: Yes, I broke my foot the last day of shooting. The last day of filming the wrestling we were fighting tigers, and I got thrown out of the ring, hitting Burt Young's chair. I fractured my left foot. I knew something broke even though the audience was roaring and chanting. I knew I broke my foot, but I climbed back into the ring. I was hopping around, while Robert was yelling, "Great job!" I was surprised because it seemed like I had really injured myself. He thought I was acting, but I wasn't acting. I continued to do the wrestling. It wasn't until the end of the day that I said, "I think my left foot is broken." I went to the hospital, and they X-rayed my foot. They said, "You have a break beneath your toes, cracked all the way down to your heel." Luckily, that was the last day of shooting. The director of photography said, "You're unbelievable. Your acting is so realistic." He's the only one I told, "I think I broke my foot." He laughed. I didn't say anything to Robert because I didn't want to get into trouble. I'm still scared.

Chris: How was it working with Peter Falk?

Laurene: Peter Falk was really strange. He was funny, and we had a great rapport. He was always talking with himself in his trailer. He was always talking to the wall, while reciting his lines. He would talk to whatever was in his room at the time. He was wonderful to work with. He had a wonderful sense of humor. He was as terrified to fly as I was. We sat in the back of the airplane. I said, "Planes don't back into mountains," and that's why I wanted to sit in the back. Everybody else sat in first class, but Peter and I would sit in the back with his assistant. I got him a watch and gave it to him at Christmas time in the back of the plane. I said, "Where's my Christmas present, you cheap son of a bitch?" I didn't expect anything. He was a wonderful person and crazy as hell. He constantly changed the dialogue in the movie and got in trouble for it by Robert. One instance, we were shooting in Ohio. The day before, Peter changed our dialogue completely, saying, "Here's your new script for tomorrow." I said to Peter, "We already memorized our lines." He just said, "No, these are your new lines. We changed it. It'll be okay. Don't worry about it." I said, "I don't think it's going to be okay, Peter." The next day we're shooting inside a restaurant. We had a rehearsal and Robert Aldrich said nothing. We're saying all of this dialogue that had nothing to do with the script at all. Robert just stared at us and said, "Cut." Peter Falk is smiling away. Robert says, "You, you and you in the alley now." We all went into the alley. Vicky and I are hanging on to each other. We thought we were going to get fired for sure because we had only been shooting maybe three or four weeks. Robert points to Vicky and me, saying, "You and you are fired. You can call your agents. If you ever betray my trust and don't follow the script the way it's written you're fired." He grabs Peter and puts him against the wall. He says, "You motherfucker! You motherfucker! I'm going to fire your ass too. Now, the three of you get back in there and do it the way it's supposed to be done." We did. That night, I went up to Robert's trailer and his wife answered the door. I said, "I'm sorry to bother you, but may I talk to Mr. Aldrich?" Robert came to the door and I said, "I want you to know I'm very sorry for what happened today. I apologize. It'll never happen again." He said, "It had nothing to do with you. I was just trying to make you two an example. I wanted to scare that fool into thinking you two would get fired. Don't think I don't know what went on. Don't think I'm so stupid that I don't know who changed the script." I said, "I'm not reporting on him." Robert said, "Of course you're not reporting on him. I'm just telling you that I know what happened. I'm not stupid. You did a very good job today, and I'm very proud of you." I thanked him and ran down to the elevator.

Photo courtesy of Laurene Landon.

Chris: How did you put your wrestling experience to use in *Hundra*?

Laurene: I always felt fearless. There are a lot of stunts on *Hundra* that obviously have nothing to do with wrestling. I would do anything, though. I didn't care about getting hurt. I felt invincible. I didn't think anything was ever going to happen to me. Any stunt they gave me, including the stunts that the stuntmen said they were afraid to do. I would call them girly girls. They said they didn't want to do the stunts, so I said I wanted to do all the stunts myself. At first, Matt Cimber said, "No, you're not doing all your own stunts." I did them all except one fall. The only one I didn't do was the fall backwards, crashing through the roof. They wouldn't let me do that stunt. I wanted to do that stunt, but I did do every other stunt in the film. The wrestling came in handy because I was so limber that I couldn't get hurt.

Chris: There was a fight scene in *Hundra* with you and the guy who couldn't stop belching and farting. Didn't you help coordinate that fight?

Laurene: Pretty much, yeah. How did you know that? At first, it was so bland. When he pulls my hair back and tries to rape me, that was in the script. They just wanted me to bang off the walls. I thought it was so stupid. I told them, "Let me jump up on the rafters and kick him. Is it OK to try some of these wrestling stunts that I talked to the stuntman about?" They went along with it. Some of the stunts were with the whip. I kept telling the actor, "Actually throw me into the wall until I bleed." That's what we did. I pretty much choreographed that scene myself. Jumping off the roof, that was scary. That was a wrestling move when I dove on the bad guy after kicking him through the building. They had a double, but I told them I was doing it myself. I did it twice. I remember diving over the director of photography twice. They were careful that I didn't land on the camera. Because of the wrestling experience jumping off the ropes and diving, I could plan exactly where I was going to land. I used my training from the wrestling days to find the spot. They were terrified that I was going to kill myself. When I was swinging back and forth on the tower, it was Thanksgiving Day and I was screaming, "It's Thanksgiving Day. How come I'm committing suicide?" Some of the crew told me the harness could have broken at any moment. I was swinging like a pendulum. I swung so far out that I was swinging past the boxes that were below me, meaning if the harness would have broken, I'm hitting the cement. Everybody laughed, thinking I was joking. That was fun, though.

Chris: You used a variety of weapons in *Hundra*. How much training were you given with each?

Laurene: With the knives it was maybe three days. I had been riding horses all my life. I loved doing the movie because I was on horseback. I love animals. They didn't want me jumping. They were scared I wasn't going to be able to jump. I said, "I've been jumping for years. I even trained for the jumps based on the script I had read so many times." Matt said, "No, you can't do this. I want a stuntman." I argued, "I'm doing this myself." My double was much heavier than myself. She was getting angrier and angrier with me because she was on the sidelines doing nothing. I wanted it be believable and natural. If you watch the movie closely, you'll see there are no cuts when I do the stunts.

Chris: How about the bow and arrow?

Laurene: That's easy. I had been a marksman all my life. I never shot animals, though. The bow and arrows probably took an hour.

Chris: In regards to the larger fight scenes, such as the opening and, later, slow motion scene, how long did you get to film them?

Laurene: Probably one or two days max. I think the opening one took about a week to shoot because there were so many extras and a lot going on. The amount always varied based on how much daylight we had, how coordinated the fight scenes were, and weather permitted. Sometimes it would snow and be freezing. There were so many things that had to be laid out, like how he wanted the bodies positioned. Everything was contingent on what the director's vision was at the time.

Chris: There's a long, violent sequence in *Hundra* done in slow motion. In your opinion, what result does the slow motion have?

Laurene: I thought it was terrible. I thought it was a waste of time, and it took away from the excitement of the moment. It was a rip-off of some Sam Peckinpah movie. I didn't notice until I saw the movie.

The one time I saw the movie, I wasn't happy with it at all. I thought it looked corny, cheesy and stupid. That's my opinion.

Chris: You've only seen the movie once?

Laurene: I've only seen it one time. That's it. I did sit through it piece by piece for the commentary, so I guess you could say I saw it twice. I hate seeing my movies. I hate looking at myself on screen. I always have. Orson Welles was the same way, not that I can compare myself to Orson Welles.

Chris: What was the one time you saw it?

Laurene: I saw it at the premiere.

Chris: A lot has been written about *Hundra* making a feminist statement. Do you think *Hundra* makes a feminist statement?

Laurene: The theme of the movie was the dawn of women's civilization. It was showing that women do have power. The objective of the director was to empower women. They can be strong, and we weren't even the weaklings back then. We are to this day, expected to be, including getting less salaries in any vocation we pursue. Matt wanted us to feel empowered and be strong. I think that's the message that came across in the movie.

Chris: You make the comment on the commentary track, "Death of their love is measured by their suffering." Can you explain that quote?

Laurene: That's a general statement. The deeper you suffer for something, in my rational mind at the time, meant that's the barometer on how much you love somebody. The worse you are treated, the more you love someone. The more you suffer, the more you love. It was a twisted statement that I made, because I don't feel that way anymore.

Chris: Despite all of the action in the film, what did you think of at least one trailer that advertised it as an "erotic adventure?"

Laurene: I think that was more an endeavor to entice, by the producers of the movie. I didn't feel it was an erotic movie at all. There's nothing erotic about it at all. Whoever put it in there did so to attract a larger audience.

Chris: I think this one was for the DVD release. It was strange because it was mostly comprised of beautiful women shots. It wasn't until the end of the trailer that they showed a sparse amount of action. Having seen the movie, it wasn't fitting. I was curious what your reaction was.

Laurene: I'm sure it was to attract a male audience to rent the video. If you look at most videos, there's a guy with a gun. Guns sell. Women are attracted to strong, tough men. There's always a guy holding a gun. Whether it's a phallic symbol, which I think it is, or a tough symbol, which I also think it is, women are attracted to that. There's a large audience that equates a gun with masculinity. The same goes for half naked women with sexuality. I'm sure that's why it's mentioned.

Chris: The tagline for the trailer also called it a "ladies only Conan." What do you think it has in common with the Conan character?

Laurene: Let me preface this by saying that when they were doing *Red Sonja* (1985), I met with Arnold Schwarzenegger and Dino DeLaurentis. They were looking for a female Conan. They didn't know that I had done *Hundra*. When I went to the Hilton to meet them, I said I had just done a movie in Spain where I played a female Conan. Arnold said to me, "You ripped off my movie." I said, "I didn't rip off your movie. I was hired to do a female Conan movie." We talked for a little while. Dino said, "There's no point in auditioning you because you've already done this movie." Dino talked like he wasn't going to do *Red Sonja* after hearing about *Hundra*. Arnold said, "Do it anyway because their movie will never match my movie." It was very similar. It was a female version of *Conan the Barbarian* (1982). That's what I've called it over the years. I was very forthright about it. Matt would say something else, but it was a rip-off of *Conan the Barbarian*. It's pretty obvious. As far as the differences go, a woman instead of a man. We shot in the same countries as they shot

66

Conan the Barbarian. Our movie was pretty much the same thing, only with a vagina instead of a penis.

Chris: Were you comfortable doing the nude scene?

Laurene: No, not at all. I had done a scene in *All the Marbles*. Robert told us, "You have to have your tops ripped off." Vicky and I didn't let our tops get ripped off. We covered ourselves with the mud while the girls were trying to rip our tops off. They did rip our tops off, but our heads were buried in the mud. Robert saw the footage and cussed us out, threatening to fire us because we didn't show our boobs. The set had been struck; they had torn it down that night. He said we were going to redo the mud wrestling scene anyway because we were a couple of liars who didn't do the topless stuff that we were going to do. We were trying to outsmart the director, but it didn't work out that way. Vicky found these panty hose that looked like flesh. I went and got them. We were practicing for the wrestling scenes. We were rehearsing, and Robert called us into his office. We were terrified because we knew what was going to happen. We had on robes, covering us down to the feet. Robert said, "You can call your manager and you can call your agent. You're both fired. You disrespected me again. I know you're both wearing those fucking panty hose. I'm not stupid. The reflection of the panty hose is casting a shadow. If you don't take off those panty hose, you're both fired right now. You can both be replaced." I said, "But this is the last scene of the movie. This is just the wrestling, remember?" He said, "I don't care. You both can be fired. Get those panty hose off!" He wanted the close up shots for the flesh and sexiness.

Chris: In *Hundra*, wasn't there a double that did the nude scene first?

Laurene: There was a double who did the nude scene, but she was short and heavy. They had her in the water because I wasn't going to show my boobs. She was maybe five-feet-five. I think Matt Cimber did that on purpose to get me to do that nude scene in the water. I saw the footage of that and said, "That's not me. My ass isn't that big. I'll do it myself." The next day we shot it, where I ride the horse in the water. The horse wasn't trained and had never been in the water. The horse was fine, at first, but then he kicked me off. Then the horse kicked me in the head, knocking me unconscious. They had to rush me to the hospital, but I did do that scene. I don't think you can see anything because it was dark during the sunset.

Chris: Tell me about going up against the dwarf in *Hundra*.

Laurene: That was one of my favorite things to do. He absolutely stole the movie. I tell everyone to this day that the little dwarf stole the movie. It was hilarious, and I couldn't stop laughing. I had to be serious, but I kept laughing. He was riding, what, a caterpillar? Then he was coming at me. It was supposed to be funny, and I hope a lot of people laughed. Matt got angry because I couldn't stop laughing. It was really, really fun, especially when he bounced off the rock. That wasn't supposed to happen and was an accident. His head pops up, and he falls down. Nobody thought that was going to happen, and it didn't happen in rehearsals.

Chris: Why do you think Hundra restrains from killing him but not other men who attack her?

Laurene: Probably because I felt sorry for him. I just couldn't believe someone of miniature stature was coming at me. My character felt there was no competition, so why waste my time? He didn't violate me, rape me, try to kill me, and he didn't try to kill any members of my family. What was the point? What did he do to me? That's how my character interpreted that guy.

Chris: There are rumors that Matt was rewriting the script on set. How chaotic, if at all, did this make the shoot?

Laurene: John wrote the script, but Matt would change things periodically. It wasn't that often. He would change a little bit of dialogue around, but we pretty much stuck to the script. It was supposed to be an action movie that would translate well in European countries, which is why it was made. People go to a lot of these movies for the action. That's why they do so well in the foreign countries. Action translates. Fire, explosions, and car chases translate everywhere. I don't understand why people go year after year to see these movies. They know they're going to see the same thing over again.

Chris: In *Yellow Hair and the Fortress of Gold*, why is it you seem to be covered up so much more than in *Hundra*?

Laurene: I think that was the character. I was half Apache and those were the clothes they wore in that period. I was using my mind, and it was more of a comedy. *Yellow Hair and the Fortress of Gold* didn't do as well as *Hundra*. He wanted me to use my mind more than sexuality or showing a lot of skin. That was the costume that they wore in that period. I didn't care one way or another as long as I have some clothes on.

Chris: You said you did most of the stunts in *Hundra*. How much of the stunts have you done in all of your films?

Laurene: Out of all the films I've done, I would say ninety-nine percent were done by me. I would never want to be doubled. It was up to what the director and stunt coordinator would say, but I would demand and insist that I do the stunt on my own. I wanted the believability to be in place so people could see that I actually did the stunts myself.

Chris: Other than the incidents we've talked about, have you ever been injured on set?

Laurene: In *Yellow Hair and the Fortress of Gold*, I was badly injured. There were a couple of incidents with the stagecoach scenes. I had flown my mom from California to Spain, so she could see Spain with me. My mother was yelling at Matt because I did the stunts where I'm being dragged by the horse and land on the stagecoach boards. I did that eleven times. I wanted to do it more and more each time, even though Matt said the first one was fine. I became too confident with myself. It became too easy for me. Matt could see that, but I couldn't see it. I was out of control, and doing the stunt became a danger issue. The stunt coordinator kept telling me I could get killed any second. The horses could kick me in the head or any sort of accident could happen. What did happen is that I was on the stagecoach and we were up in the mountains. I was on top of the stagecoach, and the horses were obviously ahead of us. I was pretending to whip the horses. The horses had gone one way to the right over an incline. The stagecoach collapsed on my legs. I thought my legs were cut off. I was screaming, but they were shooting from faraway. Everybody ran over. I kept screaming, "I think my legs are cut off!" It took seven or eight people to lift up that stagecoach. I really thought my legs were severed, especially my left leg. I had no feeling in my legs, but they were fine.

Chris: Speaking of that, you make a comment on your website about feeling the residual pain from doing the action films. Can you go into detail on that?

Laurene: Oh, yeah. I have pain in my right hip from the wrestling days. My rheumatologist said the injury in my right hip is consistent with a sports injury. I thought I had bone cancer, so we had an MRI. The pain has been so excruciating. The MRI just showed I had severe damage to my right hip and severe tendonitis and osteoarthritis on the right side. I remember when I was wrestling and doing stunts, I always favored landing on my right side. I don't why I did it that way. Maybe it's like how right-handed people only use their right hand? I always land on my right side when I was rehearsing or doing stunts. To this day my hip is still aching, and I'm in physical therapy now. I'm still very athletic, but, in retrospect, I can't believe I did all that stuff that I did. Maybe I could still do it? I haven't tried, other than beating up a few guys here and there.

Chris: *Armed Response* (1986) had a great, but male dominated, cast. How was filming that action film different from the ones where you got to be the main bad ass?

Laurene: I had a small role. I didn't have to read for it at all. They just called me and asked me if I wanted to do it. I asked them to send me the script, and I'm still a bad ass in it, of course. I still got to shoot the gun and do some action. It was just a smaller part. I wish it was a bigger part and more to do in it, but they called me to do it. I thought it was okay, and I didn't have to take my clothes off. Over the years, I lost a lot of movies because I wouldn't take my clothes off. I was asked by *Playboy* and *Hustler* if I wanted to do a layout. They were going to pay me well, but I said I wouldn't do it. I always had this thing about doing nudity. I've always been embarrassed. My parents were alive at the time, and I didn't want to embarrass my father. He didn't want me in show business in the first place because he didn't want me to get hurt emotionally. He hated the industry and was very angry with me. When I got into the business, he didn't talk to me for two years. (Avoiding) nudity isn't just for the parents. I've always been sexually repressed. I've always been terrified of being naked or topless. I'm the same way today and impossibly shy. When *Playboy* interviewed me, they wanted to do a layout. The writer told me of the layout, "Well, you're so crazy that we want to do one tennis shoe on, one off..." I said, "Do I have to be naked?" She said, "Absolutely." They were going to pay me a lot of money, 2 or $300,000. I said, "Can I wear a nightgown?" She said, "No, you can't wear a nightgown." I asked if I could, "Cover up my little girl? Wear pasties or something..." She said, "Oh, no. Some of the biggest stars have done nudity. This will only help your career." I kept trying to strike a deal where I kept my clothes on. She kept turning me down, pitching funny stuff that could be done with the nudity. She saw me as a comedian. Ultimately, I told them, "No." Both of my parents have passed away now, but I still don't think I'd do nudity today. I do that scene in *Hundra* and that little scene in *All the Marbles* and my father was furious, but he never saw *Hundra*.

Chris: Did you have any idea that *Maniac Cop* (1988) would become such a cult classic?

Laurene: No, not at all. I thought it would be on a double bill. I had no idea it would become the cult film it's become. I get so much fan mail from all over the world for my movies. Most of the mail I get is for three movies—*All the Marbles, Hundra,* and *Maniac Cop.* It is endless. I try to respond to people as best I can, but I simply can't. I had no idea whatsoever.

Chris: What are your favorite moments from *Maniac Cop?*

Laurene: Any scene with Bruce Campbell. I had a big, raging crush on Bruce. He was married, so nothing happened. Then he got divorced and we had dinner, but I had lost interest by then. It was years later.

Chris: In *Maniac Cop 2* (1990), unlike Bruce Campbell, you get a great death scene. Can you tell me about filming that sequence and what it meant for you?

Laurene: I was really pissed off at the director, Bill Lustig. They had told me I wasn't going to die. Bill Lustig was angry with me because I had a tendency to be a jokester on set. I played tricks on everybody and goofed off. I would tell everybody that it's a wrap early in the morning or lunch time. In *Maniac Cop 2*, I would call Bill "Busty, Busty," because he was very heavy-set. He got really angry. I think that's why they killed me off because I don't remember reading in the script that I was killed off at all. It was a great scene, though, with the chainsaw. At the time, I was with Christian Brando. I had bought Christian a chainsaw for Christmas. Using the chainsaw was easy because I knew how to work it. When my neck was snapped, they said I was coming back in the third one. I was going to be in the hospital. The audience would think I was dead, but I'd be coming back in part three. Obviously, I did not. They are talking about a fourth one now that I'd be in, but I don't know.

Chris: You recently attended a *Maniac Cop* reunion. Can you describe that experience?

Laurene: Bill Smith was there, God bless him. It was great to see Robert Z'Dar, but he had a bit of a health problem and was in a wheel chair. It was great to see Bill Lustig. We did the *Maniac Cop* reunion, but I

Laurene Landon poses with fellow *Maniac Cop* actors William Smith
and Robert Z'Dar. Photo courtesy of Laurene Landon.

was very disillusioned and disconcerted that Bruce Campbell didn't
join us. I guess he's too big for us and did a one-man show later that
day. He was very funny, but he wouldn't have anything to do with
any of us. I think if I had gone up to talk to him he would've talked
to me because we had that sort of rapport. I just watched him do his
one man show. The audience loved him because he has a brilliant
sense of humor. His mind is as quick as Robin Williams. We had
a wonderful reunion together. I was happy to see the cast members.
It was a bad experience in the sense that I was shooting a movie at
the time called *Drive* (2011). I had told the promoters that I didn't
think I could make the show at all, but it turned out my work ended.
I called them back and we were supposed to be put in the side of the
entrance, but they put all our tables out by the fire exit. It was so far
to the left that when you walk in that people didn't know to come
to the left to see us. They didn't see us until we did the interview. Joe
Bob Briggs told the audience where we were. Then, people came and
mobbed our tables. The first two days nobody knew where we were.

It was wonderful to see other people from the movie. I felt bad for Robert Z'Dar because his health was so bad.

Chris: In *Masters of Horror: Pick Me Up* (2006), you play a character who has a great discussion about the treatment of women. What is your point of view on this discussion?

Laurene: Nowadays, I believe what I said. In my twenties and thirties, I had the opposite approach. I used to get beaten by Christian Brando all the time. I stayed with him because I was in love, or so I thought. He had wonderful qualities. He was very sensitive and loved animals like myself. When I said those comments to Fairuza Balk, I really meant what I said. Anyone who hits me once won't hit me again. I've never been abused by a man after my relationship with Christian was over. I could tell a man's temper by how he treated waiters and how he drove in traffic. Early on, I could tell that someone who cusses in traffic was not someone who I want to be with. They are potential abusers. With Christian, I would tolerate that, but not after my relationship with him ended.

Chris: What have you learned from Larry Cohen?

Laurene: Larry Cohen is the greatest human being I've ever met in my life. What I've learned from him is to let it go in one ear and out the other. He's a brilliant historian about any movie ever made. He knows every character. We've watched many old movies together. Without him, I wouldn't have watched or learned from them. He's, bar none, the greatest male I've ever met, except for my father of course.

Chris: You've been shopping around a script centering on a dog pound. What inspired this?

Laurene: My love for animals. I contribute to an organization called Circle L. I go there every Christmas and spend time with my friends that run the ranch. I love animals and think puppy mills are one of the greatest horrors of human civilization today. The people who buy thousand-dollar animals should be put down themselves. I'll get a lot of terrible feedback because people buy these animals, but it just makes me sick when animals are begging in shelters. I was fixated on trying to end puppy mills and saving animals that have no voice or choice. If you've been to a shelter then you know how terrible it is. I wrote this movie in 2002. Originally it was called *Dog Pen*, as in penitentiary. I wrote it as a drama and the studios loved it, but they said nobody would see it when a puppy mill is involved. They wanted me to make it into a comedy.

Chris: Who would you consider to be a Bad Ass Woman of Cinema?

Laurene: At this point, I would say Sandra Bullock. I have never met her, but she epitomizes strength within women who have to rise against adversity. She rose above how she was treated in her marriage. She came out smiling instead of eliciting pity for herself. She plays strong, tough women. I feel the same way about Bette Davis. She's always been an icon and pillar of strength. I feel like Sandra Bullock is the same way. Both of those women are tremendous. A bad ass woman of cinema depicts courage and self-respect. They have to use their heart and mind, not just their fists.

Photo courtesy of Marrie Lee.

MARRIE
LEE

Marrie Lee is living a Cinderella story. Both of Marrie's parents died when she was young. Marrie was only sixteen, working as a receptionist in a nightclub, when she came across an ad for a movie role that would change her life. Marrie got the role, beginning a long professional relationship with Bobby Suarez. The two of them developed the iconic, butt-kicking, martial arts maiden that is Cleopatra Wong. *They Call Her... Cleopatra Wong* (1978) introduced the world to an Asian, female James Bond. The campy, over-the-top action scenes famously include Marrie in a nun outfit, firing a unique, four-barrel shotgun, and gunfire from her motorcycle mowing down lines of bad guys. The popularity of the character resulted in Cleopatra Wong returning for two more movies. The second film, *Devil's Three* (1979), has her teaming up with a flamboyant Franco Guerrero and an obese woman named Rotunda. The third film, *Dynamite Johnson* aka *The Return of Bionic Boy* (1989), teamed Cleopatra up with another unique character. Despite the success of this character, Marrie would walk away from movies. Since 1989, Marrie has become a successful businesswoman, running her own health care company in Singapore. The Cleopatra Wong series continue to screen around the world, get rereleased in new formats, and build a new legion of fans.

Notable roles
They Call Her…Cleopatra Wong
Devil's Three
Dynamite Johnson

Chris: Tell me about your childhood.

Marrie: I was born in a little clinic in Singapore Chinatown on November 25, 1959. I was born overdue and weighed a hefty nine pounds. My parents, who already had my brother and sister, initially weren't prepared for another baby, and my mum even took some Chinese herbs to prevent the pregnancy when I was less than two months in her womb. I was a survivor even before I saw the light of day. I adored my father, and from a toddler would learn things just to earn his praise. I would have been a brilliant academician if my dad did not pass away when I was six. I remember walking the corridor outside my home like a zombie an hour after my mum had told me my dad died in the ambulance on the way to hospital. I just couldn't cry and was in denial. It was only when a neighbor stopped me in my tracks that I just bawled out, and I couldn't stop for hours.

We were very poor then. My dad, a construction company manager, was the only breadwinner, and my brother had just barely landed his first job at eighteen. My mum had to go out and work for the first time in her life. She had to take on jobs like canteen helper and domestic worker just to put dinner on the table and see me through school.

I alternated between being the best and the worst student in school. There was this streak of rebelliousness in me. I had won the top math student award in the entire grade six classes, but I had also received a two weeks suspension from class for playing truant. I had been a teacher's pet, and I had been a teacher's nightmare. I was a person of extremes at times. It took me years to moderate and calm the rebel in me. It broke my heart when my mum followed my dad. I was sixteen, and, in order to survive, I had to join the workforce.

I loved acting from the time I was a toddler and had playacted with every towel, bed sheet, blanket, and dingly dangly bling bling I could lay my hands on. I loved Cantonese opera and would sing along with my favorite opera stars on the radio or TV. I had often enough told my mum I will be an actress one day.

Chris: What influenced you as a child?

Marrie: I read any Enid Blyton book I could lay my hands on. That could account for the "naughtiest girl in school" reputation I had. I have very colorful vivid dreams and recall. I lived Enid Blyton in my dreams. I believed in pixies and gnomes and toys that came alive when I sleep. I believed in fairy tales and miracles. I believed in life after death and that there is always a reason for things happening. I like retelling stories and jokes—I like to entertain. I have always wanted to be an entertainer of sorts, so it probably didn't come as a surprise when I got into showbiz. It was in my blood all along.

Chris: Before you got into acting, what type of woman were you?

Marrie: Naïve, inexperienced, and a typical goblok. I was eager to please and learn. They call me a "director's actress" as anything the director says I will do without question. I remember the gun target practice scene in *They Call Her... Cleopatra Wong*. In between takes, when they were moving the cameras, I was still in position with the gun in hand, in a half squat, not daring to move till someone mocked and said, "You don't have to be so hard working Cleo. Come on and take a rest." The crew liked me because I put on no airs, and was never a prima donna. I was down to earth and friendly—attributes that follow me up to this day.

Photo courtesy of Marrie Lee.

Chris: What characteristics do you believe make up a Bad Ass woman?

Marrie: Oh, she must be sexy and beautiful with a touch of meanness in her. That makes all the ass kicking movies so watchable. Look at my favorites Milla Jovovich and Uma Thurman. They are beautiful, extremely sexy, and intense.

Chris: Unlike a lot of films, *They Call Her...Cleopatra Wong* has several iconic moments: the large fight scenes, nun with a large gun, and the gun-loaded motorcycle to name a few. What are some favorite moments from your career?

Photo courtesy of Marrie Lee.

Marrie: During the filming of *Dynamite Johnson*, we filmed for forty-eight hours straight at a mining camp. The miners and their families came to watch the shooting; there were easily 300 of them. Through the forty-eight hours they were the ones who helped me overcome the tiredness with their constant cheering of "Cleo! Cleo!" It was really uplifting. There were some behind the scenes, which the audience did not get to watch. In *They Call Her...Cleopatra Wong*, we were shooting in the Chinese Gardens in Singapore. You know what they say about wrestlers being the best actors. These wrestlers I worked with were comical. After I had fought and killed a couple of them, they were supposed to lay still and play dead. Instead, they sat up and smiled at the camera. They would jump in the air to pounce on Cleo like Superman, taking off with both arms raised and fists clenched. They only needed the blue and red suit. Such scenes were endearing to me.

Chris: What training did you have to go through to play Cleopatra Wong?

Marrie: I was assigned a personal martial arts trainer the moment I set foot on the Philippines. He was Alex Pecate, a 6th Dan Karate expert and his father was running the martial arts school at the YMCA Manila. We did a lot of our training there. Incidentally, Alex also played the Interpol agent who was killed at the end of *They Call Her…Cleopatra Wong*. Although his background was in karate, he also coached me in Judo, Taekwondo and Arnis Sticks. I also had a motorbike trainer who taught me some stunt-riding like doing wheelies and balancing on a bike.

Also, during that era, a famous Filipino actor, Fernando Poe Jr. wowed the audience with his single-hand cocking of the .22 caliber gun so Bobby decided I must be the first woman doing it. And not just doing from the ground but in the air, so I was made to practice on the trampoline with a gun thrown to me. I had to catch it, cock it in the air singlehandedly, and shoot before my feet reach the ground. I have a scar still on my right hand pinkie where the flesh was torn off during one such practice.

Chris: Where did the idea for the gun at the end of *They Call Her… Cleopatra Wong* come from?

Marrie: Just like in every James Bond movie where there is some special gadget, Bobby wanted the same for his movies in *They Call Her… Cleopatra Wong*. We had this four-barrel shotgun in addition to a bow and arrow with explosive heads, which I used to blow up the helicopter at the finale. In *Dynamite Johnson*, it is upgraded to a one piece shot gun that could be transformed to a bow and arrow with explosives. In *Devil's Angels* (1979), we had a five-barrel shotgun with the ability to shoot a single arrowhead bullet with a rope attached, so I can shoot at a wall and embed the bullet in the wall to scale it from another building. I think these gadgets were quite innovative thirty-five years ago, although it is commonplace now. All I can say is that Bobby is extremely creative and far sighted.

Chris: How was it to handle and fire?

Marrie: Handling and firing the gun was not the problem. We used blanks for our filming and there was hardly any recoil. What I do not like is the gun powder burns on the face after every shot. Sometimes you see actors flinch when shooting a gun. It is not fear of the shooting but the anticipation of the pain from the burns.

Chris: How did the role change your life?

Marrie: It did, big time. It fulfilled the ambition and dream of a little girl playing with towels and blankets. It made me and Singapore an international name in the movie industry. I suppose you can say that Cleopatra Wong is textbook theory for our local students of filming, as there are not many Singapore movies that really make it around the world. I have collected so many posters of my movies from around the world, printed in Spanish, German, Turkish, Yugoslavian, Arabic, and French. You can't deny the international heritage of the Cleopatra Wong movies.

Chris: When you saw the ad for the audition, did you hesitate for any reason?

Marrie: Not one bit. At that time, I had already played a small role in a Hong Kong movie, and I was hungry for more opportunities.

Chris: Tell me about the audition process for the role of Cleopatra Wong.

Marrie: I answered an ad with the heading "Are you sexy, seductive and smart?" I asked my sister, Betty, to accompany me for the initial interview. I was told that I was required to go back for another interview when the producer and director was in town. That was when I met Bobby Suarez. I had already seen the artist impression of how Cleopatra Wong will look like, so I was dressed in a blouse and mini-skirt, with a wide-brimmed hat and boots. I could ride a bike and had some martial arts training from my brother, Jimmy. Bobby Suarez, the producer and director, was a little curt at the interview and said they would contact me if I was successful. I honestly did not think I was going to get the role. A month later, I received a letter saying I was to play Cleopatra Wong. A week later, Bobby came to Singapore to bring me to Manila.

Chris: How did you come to get the name Marrie Lee?

Marrie: Bobby said that Doris Young was not a glamorous name and wanted to give me a screen name. Bruce Lee was a world phenomenon at that time so it was logical to be a "Lee." To make it rarer, Marie was spelled with a double "R," so I became Marrie Lee.

Chris: You considered yourself "plumpish" at the time. What do you think this added to your character and in the way she is viewed?

Marrie: Well, you don't have to be skinny to be an accomplished actress. Beauty is very subjective. Some like it skinny while others like actresses with a bit of meat and curves on them. Of course, modern day advertising denotes that beauty must be thin while olden art shows that plump women are preferred. Mona Lisa was not a thin woman. I think the most important thing is if you can effectively live the role you are asked to play. Cleopatra Wong is an Interpol agent and requires someone more athletic and agile. I think at that point of time, I was probably regarded as rugged and built solid, not waif like. Of course, it doesn't help that one always appears to be fifteen to twenty percent heavier on the big screen. But there are great actresses of all shapes and sizes and looks.

Chris: How much of your stunt work did you do?

Marrie: Bobby was a very persuasive man. He would tell me that they could get a stuntman to play me, but the cameras would be closely focused and people may see that it is not me, so I always replied I would do it. Of course, there were extremely dangerous scenes where I was not professionally trained to do my stunts so that I had to allow someone to stand in. I think I used the most stand-ins in the filming of *Dynamite Johnson* because I had an appendix operation and was supposed to take three months rest from excessive action scenes.

Chris: What are some injuries you received from filming?

Marrie: During the filming of *Dynamite Johnson*, I also had a bad fall running on the rocky hillside slope, resulting in a wrist fracture that pushed the bone out of position. But then, Johnson Yap was in the Philippines during his six-week school holidays, and filming had to go on. I never got time to recuperate from my injuries and my left wrist stayed a bit twisted. I had cuts behind the knees from jumping through real glass and other sprains and minor injuries.

Chris: What was the most dangerous stunt you performed?

Marrie: Well, I lived to tell the tale. In *Dynamite Johnson*, I hung from a helicopter 100 feet without a safety belt or net. The first and third take was okay, but during the second take, right after I put my foot in the loop, I hung on to the rope at mid-level instead of straight above my head. The moment the helicopter lifted I was suspended at a horizontal angle. I shouted for them to put me down, but the sound from the helicopter drowned all my screams. It took all I had to support my body weight with my hands. If I let go, I would have fallen to my death. I had to endure it for more than seven minutes before they lowered me down.

Chris: What was Bobby Suarez like as a director? What did he bring to the movies that others did not?

Marrie: Bobby was a genius and geniuses are known to be eccentric and temperamental—that was what Bobby could be. He would try out new ideas, sometimes, to the point of disregarding continuity. In one scene for *Dynamite Johnson*, I was wearing an Afro wig I bought earlier. Bobby liked it on me and said to shoot the next scene with me wearing the wig. So it was long hair in one scene, Afro the next and back to long hair again. Quite comical.

I was taught taekwondo and karate. When we were shooting in Hong Kong, suddenly Bobby wanted me to fight Chinese kung fu style, and he asked the Hong Kong martial arts director to do a kung fu routine. I had to learn kung fu styles within the day. It was quite funny because I thought I was doing eagle style until the martial arts director said that it looked more like chicken claws.

Photo courtesy of Marrie Lee.

Bobby always liked an international cast in his movies to give it the feel of an international movie. With the small budget he had, he would persuade Caucasian tourists, backpackers to act for free or perhaps for meals and transport, but the cast and crew always had fun. These days, a lot of Hollywood movies are looking towards the East for locations and cast and Bobby was doing it over thirty years ago. Sometimes I watch some current action movies and some scenes are so nostalgic—they feel like a remake of some of the scenes in my movies.

Chris: What was the rehearsal like for the fight scene at the school? Any idea how many you took on?

Marrie: The routine was thought up and created on the spot. Usually while the cameras were being moved, the martial arts director would think of the next few moves. Then I would practice with the stunt people until we are familiar, and then we started filming. In the Singapore fight scene with the wrestlers and then the martial art students, there might have been fifty fighters.

Chris: Was the exploitation aspect understood on set? For instance, you in a nun outfit with a large gun. What were your feelings towards this angle?

Marrie: I wish Bobby was still alive and I can ask him what was on his mind when he wrote the storyline of Cleopatra Wong. I think in this story plot, the inclusion of nuns captured and held captive in a convent that was producing strawberry jam would have more commercial appeal than a strawberry factory and its workers being held.

Chris: You mentioned the gun was inspired by James Bond. Was Cleopatra Wong also intended to be a female James Bond? If so, in what ways do you see it as similar and what did you try to change?

Marrie: Definitely, a female James Bond. In an era when there were not too many female heroines, a female Interpol agent following the likes of James Bond was like a surefire success. We both had the use of unconventional weapons, the cockiness, and confident personality. Probably only the many bed scenes that were a regular feature of James Bond movies were missing. There was only one bed scene that Cleo was in. It was in *They Call Her… Cleopatra Wong*, but not in the other two Cleopatra Wong movies. I think by having a sexy female agent in the movie, the sexual connotation is strong enough without resorting to the obvious.

Chris: What were your thoughts on how the character was handled sexually?

Marrie: I think apart from the obvious dress mode and camera angles that fleetingly caught glimpses of legs and breasts, it was all subtle. Of course, there was this part where Cleo Wong took off her skirt to distract the wrestlers, but, other than that, quite mild I would think.

Chris: What was it like working with Johnson Yap?

Marrie: Johnson Yap was eleven when I met him. For a kid his age, he behaved very professionally on the set and always fulfilled what he was told to do. There was a mischievous side of him too. I remember him knocking on my door at four in the morning and then running to hide. We had to leave the hotel at five, and he went around waking everyone up.

Chris: Describe the reactions of fans when they meet you.

Marrie: There had been occasions where people came up shyly to me and asked if they could take a picture with me or have my autograph. Some may be a bit more daring and asked me what it was like making the movies. I think in Singapore, people are a little more reserved and shy.

Chris: What do your family and friends think of your iconic role? How does your opinion differ now from when you began acting?

Marrie: They are all extremely proud of me and thrilled that Cleopatra Wong up to this day enjoys so much publicity and exposure. Over thirty years ago, when I made the movies, I was very critical of myself and how I performed. Now when I watch my movies again, I feel a great sense of achievement and asked myself, "Did I really do that? How can I fight so tirelessly throughout the whole movie?" I compare it to action movies made during the same period, and I can truthfully say that I did not do so badly after all. I did Singapore proud.

Chris: You continue to attend revival screenings for your films. What is that experience like?

Marrie: We did several in Singapore. Some include the Singapore International Film Fest, the Screen Singapore, and Media Fiesta in 2010 and 2011. SIA even showed it on all their flights for two months in 2008. I have also been to the Black Movie Festival in Geneva and Brisbane International Film Festival. It was a real eye opener for me that people can have so much passion for old movies when there are so many great new movies churned out every year. I can get a kick each time I hear the applause at the end of the screening, and I feel they really enjoyed the movie. I always enjoyed the Q&A session after each screening. There are always media and publicity around the events. It was indeed a treat for me each time.

Chris: Why did you not continue in acting?

Marrie: My three year contract ended with Bobby, and I was approached by a Hollywood company to do a TV pilot *Charlie Chan's No. 1 Daughter*. It would have been a TV series if the first movie took off. Unfortunately, when everything was signed and I was supposed to leave for Hollywood, the first of the infamous 1981 guild strikes began. This went on for almost a year. By the time the industry started moving again, I was married, and my husband then didn't want me to continue acting as it would have meant going overseas for long periods of time when he was in Singapore. That ended my movie career.

Chris: You went on to run your own company. Tell me about the road from acting to running your own business.

Marrie: After I came back to Singapore, it was difficult getting a good career path without qualifications so I started a paper chase. As I had the intention of doing my own business someday, I managed to get qualified in the areas that I thought essential in a business—IT, sales, marketing, accounting and finance. After spending some years in working with consumers, I got an offer for a joint venture and to run the company.

YUKARI
OSHIMA

As a child, Yukari was, not surprisingly, an athletic tomboy. Her martial arts talent started to shine in high school as she transitioned from gymnastics to karate. After winning a national karate championship, Yukari had her sights set on being a physical education teacher. Luckily, for action fans worldwide, Yukari fell in love with Hong Kong movies. A part time job as a stunt woman would mark the beginning of Yukari's career. Yukari would establish herself as an action star, acting in over seventy films. The brutal style, trademark hair, and tomboyish look brought something unique to the "girls with guns" era. Many of her films were team-ups with the adorable, yet deadly, Moon Lee. Yukari would play a mixture of heroes and villains but was always the highlight.

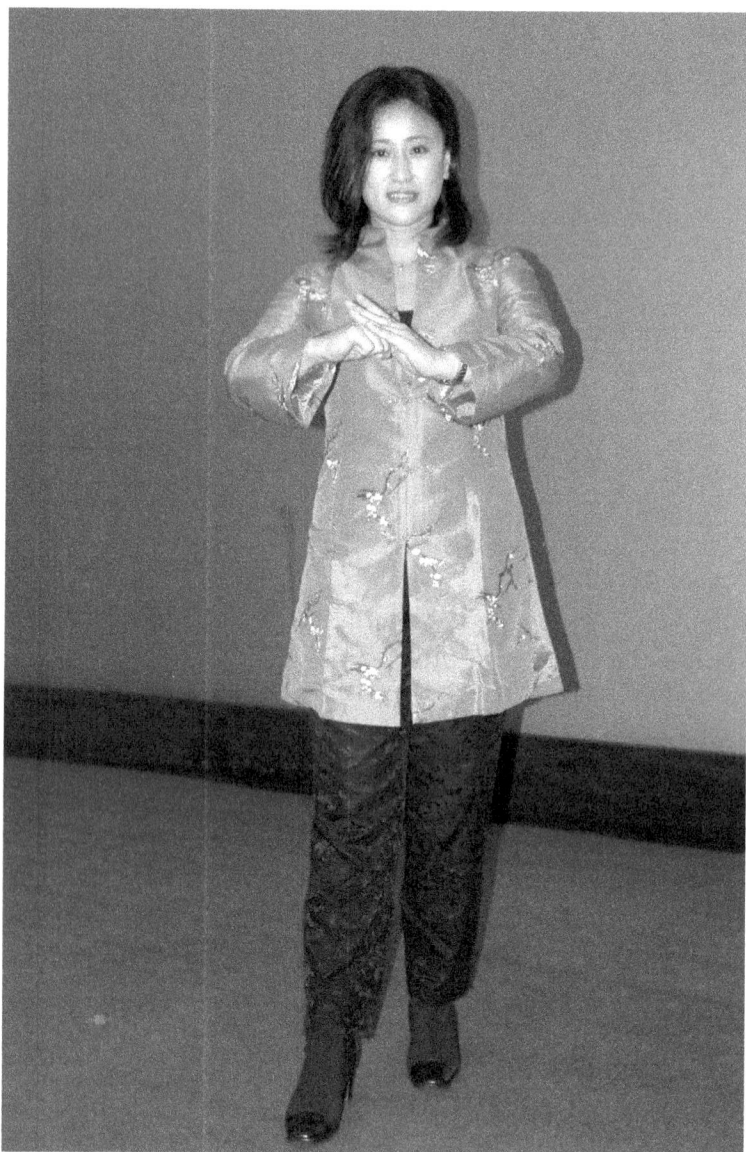

Photo courtesy of Yukari Oshima.

Yukari's films often include memorable fight scenes that are rarely seen with women fighters. Whether Yukari was taking on Moon Lee, Sophia Crawford, or a male actor, the adrenaline accelerated, and the moviegoer is pushed to the edge of their seat.

Notable roles
Outlaw Brothers
Midnight Angels
Angel Mission

Chris: How would you describe your childhood?

Yukari: I was bright, cheerful, and also recognized as a tomboy.

Chris: You practiced as a gymnast when you were a child. How do you think that the ability helped your future career as an actress?

Yukari: With the help of acrobatics, I was able to have the ability to become a good stunt woman. The art of balance and space really helped me a lot. I would say the skills I learned helped me become a good action actress.

Chris: You started studying karate in high school. What led to this decision?

Yukari: I studied from my last year in junior high school through my senior year in high school. I was a really active girl then, so my mom made me learn it to foster my concentration ability as well as an art of self-defense. Of course, at the time, I never, ever thought that it was going to help my future career. My friends inspired me to keep going despite the hard training. I also liked the very exhilarating feeling after the practice. Yeah, I really liked it.

Chris: How did you go from wanting to be a physical education teacher to acting?

Yukari: I thought being a physical education teacher in the future would let me take great advantage of my physical strength, so I went to a sport science university to get a teaching degree. However, the Hong

Kong movies I saw and a part time job as a stunt woman during my university era fully shifted my direction to an action world where I could use my talent more.

Chris: When you were starting out in acting, how did you envision your career?

Yukari: My dream then was to appear in Hong Kong movies with Yuen Biao. I was aiming to be the best stunt woman ever in the Asian region.

Chris: What are your thoughts on the "girls with guns" era?

Yukari: In the imaginative world of movies, I just think that it would be OK for women to fight like men do.

Chris: Please talk about your transition into leading a stunt team.

Yukari: First and foremost, action can't be done alone. It is necessary to have good people to understand each other. It leads to a relieved and safe job. Moreover, having my own team at my job site could save a lot of time, and my junior fellows, who have the same dream, can inherit my experience directly.

Chris: A lot of your fight scenes are brutal and well executed, yet they had to be shot very quickly. Was this a benefit of using your own team?

Yukari: Well, the short camera blocking technique is a particular culture in Hong Kong movie scene. They intend to express the dynamics of speed and power by incorporating many cuts in a scene. However the length of time used for one scene containing many quick shots was really short, but we devoted ourselves by taking the best cut over and over again, and sometimes we spent so many hours to take just one cut. We put our spirits and power concentration into one short cut. It looks like a sprint race, doesn't it?

Chris: How much physical contact was allowed during fight scenes?

Yukari: Just acting wasn't good enough to express the live fighting performance, so we were demanded to act our best. That means there were no rules about physical contact. We were very serious.

Chris: What do you consider to be your best fight scene?

Yukari: Almost all of my parts include action and fight scenes, so it is difficult to choose the best one. I could say that the acrobatic stunt and martial arts action were something I recommend.

Chris: Over the course of your career, which actress or stunt woman did you enjoy fighting with the most?

Yukari: Well, it must be Moon Lee. We worked together so many times, so we got closer in the process. She was such an attractive woman personally.

Chris: What are some of the injuries you've sustained when filming?

Yukari: Injuries are always associated with my career as an action actress. I suffered from minor injuries all the time during my career. When I hurt my face, I had troubles in putting my makeup on and connecting cuts as natural as possible. The biggest injury I had was when two ligaments in my knee got torn—I couldn't even walk. I completely recovered only after a year of rehabilitation. The fear has remained deep inside me, and I still struggle with it. However, without this fear, I wouldn't have kept my career as a stunt woman until I lost my life. I've learned how to handle myself. That's one good thing my injury brought me.

Chris: Sophia Crawford talked about the difference it made going from independent actress to signing with your team. Can you discuss what you were able to do for your fellow actors.

Yukari: Yeah, I was supporting my team members not only in the action aspect, but also in giving them advice on how to live abroad. It was tough enough for them to live in a foreign country, and they had to commit themselves to movie shootings in an unfamiliar setting. Sophia, however, was a woman with a lot of guts, and she worked hard when she was in Hong Kong. She was such a hard working person with a strong mentality, which should be admired.

Chris: In the late 1980s and early 1990s, what was the Hong Kong Cinema scene like for women?

Yukari works on a fight scene with Sophia Crawford.
Photo courtesy of Sophia Crawford.

Yukari: It was so-called the era of "Women acting in action movies in Hong Kong." Even act-oriented actresses were having bruises on their feet and screaming in the sites.

Chris: Did you ever feel like you had to work harder to earn respect because you are female?

Yukari: Well, maybe. I must've been a little careful not to bother the other actors and stuff around me in the shooting sites because I was a woman. But I guess that it didn't bother me much. I was just struggling with what I had to do then.

Chris: What was, and is, your relationship with Moon Lee like?

Yukari: We used to work together a lot, so it wasn't necessary to keep in touch with our personal lives. But I really miss her now. Yeah, I really do. I wish I could see her.

Chris: Can you explain why you started making films in the Philippines under the name Cynthia Luster?

Yukari: To tell you the truth, I just noticed later. The name change was

96

done by a buyer of the movie field in the Philippines. My name had been changed to Cynthia Luster from Yukari Oshima. By the time I knew it, I had been already known as Cynthia there. In fact, there had been some arguments during the process.

Chris: *Riki-Oh* (1991) has become a cult classic in America. There are t-shirts and constant midnight screenings. What were your thoughts on the film when you were making it?

Yukari: Having my hair cut short. . . it was hard to act out a man's part. The movie was based on a Japanese comic, and real comic books were used for the acting scripts. It was really fun, and it felt like I was in a real cartoon world. We even did the shooting in a real jail.

Chris: Are you surprised by *Riki-Oh*'s success?

Yukari: Yes, I am. I am genuinely surprised to hear that so many people saw the movie.

Chris: *Legendary Amazons* (2011) teamed you up with many talented actresses. What was the film like to work on?

Yukari: It was such an honor to costar with so many attractive actresses and being on the same stage with them. Beautiful clothing and hair accessories for a historical play had made me impressed for a couple of days since the first day of the shooting, but soon those harsh actions in the last half of the movie led me to a reality. The beautiful clothing and the hair accessory I enjoyed turned out to bother my action so much. The temperature in the inner part of Mongolia for the movie shooting finally dropped until minus twenty degree Celsius—it did hurt me a lot.

Chris: A lot of comparisons have been made between yourself and Luxia Jiang. What are your thoughts on the actress?

Yukari: I am so sorry, but I don't personally know her yet. But I am so honored to have such a person to be compared. I just wish her luck.

Chris: We met through your Action School. Please give some information about what you're doing now.

Yukari: Using my hands-on experience from my career, I want to develop action stars who can meet the director or audience's requests as well as being capable of action from this action school. I am teaching them on site with reliable instructors at Human Academy in Fukuoka.

Chris: Which of your films do you consider your best?

Yukari: Well, I think it is *Angel Mission* (1993). The best part was probably the ending full of action with Moon Lee.

Chris: Are you satisfied with your career?

Yukari: Yes, I am. There is no holding back.

Chris: Who do you consider to be a Bad Ass Woman of Cinema?

Yukari: Well, let me name two admirable actresses. Gong Li in China and Sayuri Yoshinaga in Japan. Both of them are not action actresses, though.

Chris: Thank you for your time.

Yukari: Thank you so much for taking your time. May everyone love action movies forever.

Translated by: Hiromi Kaneyuki

CHENG
PEI PEI

Nicknamed the "Queen of the Swordswomen," Cheng Pei Pei was born in Shanghai in 1946. At a young age, Pei Pei began studying ballet, learning movement that would help her become a martial arts actress. Preparing at the Shaw Brothers training course, Pei Pei would do well over twenty films for the company. One of those films, King Hu's revolutionary *Come Drink with Me* (1966), would rocket her to stardom. The success of *Come Drink with Me* led to numerous starring roles as a sword-wielding heroine. Her characters were often smart, fierce, lethal, and mistaken for men. Pei Pei was headlining one theatrical release after another until she decided to marry and leave the business. After her marriage ended, she would return to the movie business. Besides martial

THE GIRL WITH THE THUNDERBOLT KICK
Starring WANG YU CHENG PEI PEI LO LIEH CHAO HSIN-YEN

arts films, she starred in musicals like *Hong Kong Nocturne* (1966), hosted a talk show, and starred in numerous comedies. She would once again gain recognition for her villainous role in the international hit *Crouching Tiger, Hidden Dragon* (2000). Cheng Pei Pei's wide range and memorable roles have made her an acting legend.

Notable roles
Come Drink With Me
Crouching Tiger, Hidden Dragon
Lady Hermit
Golden Swallow

Chris: What was it like growing up in Shanghai in the 1950s?
Cheng Pei Pei: That was the best time in China. It just turned over.

Everything was very nice. People tried to be very gentle. It's very different from nowadays thinking. I feel like I should always do something for society, for the people, and for the country. It's more this kind of thinking. Always thinking this should be very important for your life. Even though I became an actress later on, I never spent a lot of money on a special dress or whatever. At that time, my father went to jail in Mongolia for supporting the other party. In 1949, the government changed. I'm in a very bad position because I'm not a normal farmer or poor person. People think if you come from this type of family that you should be this or that. That's why I always want to do better. Even though I come from this type of family, I can still do what you can do.

Chris: What was your relationship like with your family?

Cheng Pei Pei: We had four sisters and brothers. She was a single mother bringing us all up. Most of the time, she was doing her job making money to survive. And because of the situation with my father, that's why she moved to Hong Kong and stayed with my uncle, her brother. We could not go out together, so it was like one by one. I'm the last one because I'm the oldest. So I stayed maybe three or four years by myself in China. That's why I always think I'm responsible for my brother and sister. I am always the mother to them even though I'm only two or three years older than them. In family, I've always taken care of them. My mother was always working. We are not that close. We have very different opinion of everything.

Chris: Tell me the story about taking your sister to dance class.

Cheng Pei Pei: You know, I was eight already. My second youngest sister was five. My mother always thought she was small, flexible and active. I was very quiet when I was young. I was a few years older than the others, so I was already like a mother to them. She wanted to take her to learn dance. Of course, she's only five so she's just playing around. I'm thinking, "You spent that much money then I want to learn it for her." That's why I would just stand outside to

101

try to do whatever the teacher taught her. So the teacher asked my mother, "Why not your older daughter?" My mother says, "No, she never can be..." I continued learning and it was a lot of money to ask. It's not like now where everyone is having dance and piano lessons. I think for a long time my mother didn't think I could dance. I was pretty old after I moved to Hong Kong. One day she was suddenly like, "Oh, you know..." She called me Pei Pei. "Pei Pei can dance!"

Chris: Was she able to see you when you started doing musicals and film?

Cheng Pei Pei: Can't tell because she's not always home. Those years I think she was in Bangkok with my stepfather. I don't think she knew until she signed the contract because I'm underage. She thinks it's OK because more people can make money and survive. I don't think she thought I could be a success in this field because I'm very quiet, strange.

When I first went to Hong Kong, because I don't speak good Cantonese, I had no friends. So I went into the city that belongs to Shaw Brothers. She never thought I could become an actress. She never thought that way. But if I can earn money to help the family then she thought it was okay. She's thinking that way more than thinking I would become great success.

Chris: What was her reaction when you started to become famous?

Cheng Pei Pei: I really don't know. I think she's happy. She fought the company a few times for the money. Then they moved to Australia. So they need a lot of money to move to Australia. She talked to my company. They had all my salaries going to Australia. So, to me, it's more money things. She never pushed me very much. I always wear the clothes she doesn't wear. My mother is a very, very old fashioned woman. I don't think she really understands it. Even me, I didn't know I was very successful until after I was married and I came to the States. I had never noticed it.

Chris: Did you notice a difference in reaction to your celebrity status when you moved to America?

Cheng Pei Pei: For the Chinese society, everyone knew me. In those times, Chinese movies were only showing in Chinatown. People who went overseas to study would watch Chinese movies. In Chinatown I'm still very famous. I was not recognized in America.

Chris: Did you have ambitions as a child to be in film or be a martial artist?

Cheng Pei Pei: No, I never thought I would. I always think of myself as a ballet dancer. Since I was eight, I had been studying ballet. I love ballet. However, I'm too tall and too big for ballet dancing. It's difficult for me to even find a partner, especially where I went in Hong Kong. The guys were always very small. It made the dancing interesting. Also, as I mentioned, I was a very quiet girl, so I never imagined I would become an actress. I did martial arts because I went to the training school. They have a lot of teachers teach us all the martial arts. Because of my dance background it was easy for me to pick up. I think that's why I had the interest to learn. I love to learn new things.

Chris: How would you compare dancing with martial arts?

Cheng Pei Pei: In the beginning, I didn't notice the similarities. It wasn't until I talked to King Hu. He was the one thinking I can be a martial arts actress. I don't think it's only because of the look and that I'm a dancer. One of the girls who was a dancer too and I did a dance number that became very famous in the small circles that we performed. Jackie Chan, Sammo Hung, and that group were always there to perform with us. I actually play a guy in that number. Because we performed this with me playing a guy is why King Hu thinks I can pull off being a martial arts actress. It can be very good for a woman doing martial arts movie. He taught me that when you do dance you're still using your energy. When you do a martial art, you need to think and use a different energy to make people think you can fight. He wanted me to understand the tempo. I just did *Hong Kong Nocturne* (1967), a musical, so I learned more than just the dance from the Japanese. So, I understood the rhythm and tempo that he wanted. I understood the tempo of the martial arts better. Martial arts, when you look at it, there's a lot of power involved. Actually ballet is very strong too. But with martial arts it not only makes people think you are very strong but still feminine. If they are very tough, I don't think they can be a very good martial arts actress.

Chris: How was your dance training useful when you started in film?

Cheng Pei Pei: It's very useful. You stretch your body. I think for other people who study martial arts, it's difficult because they don't have very flexible body. The ballet routine and the martial arts routine have very similar things. The movement is different. The energy is different.

Chris: How did you get started in the martial arts?

Cheng Pei Pei: Because of movies. People think I know the martial arts, but I only know the martial arts from making movies.

Chris: Can you describe the Shaw Brothers training you attended?

Cheng Pei Pei: I think I'm very lucky to have trained with the Shaw Brothers, especially at that time. Of course, it's up to you to learn. I loved learning, so I got the chance to learn everything. Shaw Brothers gave me a chance to train. Later on, I got the chance to go to Japan to learn dance. A lot of actresses in Hong Kong never got this kind of chance to have people train you first.

Chris: What was some of the training you went through?

Cheng Pei Pei: There was a karate class. I'm one of the instructors too, teaching Chinese dance and ballet. We always had people to train. It's up to you. If you want to do it, you can.

Chris: Would you describe it as a college with a variety of athletic and artistic classes?

Cheng Pei Pei: Yeah. You can't say it's a college because that's training for the company, right? It's for the actress and actor.

Chris: Did you ever feel—positively or negatively—that you were treated differently because you were a female?

Cheng Pei Pei: No. I think I've been very lucky that I'm female. You look back at Chinese movies and they always have female as the lead until Bruce Lee became a star. Even with Jimmy Wang Yu, at the time we were equal. Still, at that time, the female was in a higher position. Not like now, where you can see the film always has a male lead.

In reality, it was very different. The women were expected to be the wife, not doing anything, but in the movies it was very different. That gave me more of a chance to get a female audience. They want to be me. They want to be a hero and fight.

Chris: How did King Hu's style differ from others?

Cheng Pei Pei: Go back to that old Chinese martial arts movie. It's more like a documentary. They were more like staged martial arts with no movement. Two people fighting there. King Hu studied both Japanese and western movies. Then, he used different angles and developed a way to present the martial arts. The Chinese martial arts movie totally changed. People think I'm the first martial arts lady. Of course, I'm not the first. The martial arts actress has been around since silent movies. You can look at *Crouching Tiger, Hidden Dragon*. It's the same but improved a lot.

Chris: Did you understand the philosophies he was putting into the film at the time of filming?

Cheng Pei Pei: He taught us. He's a very good teacher. We're not only doing acting on the set but after that with editing and so on. He taught us all the things we need to follow as students. That's why I always call him "teacher." He was teaching a lot. Why he's doing that, what's his philosophy, what he thinks of the culture…he studied a lot.

Chris: Since he was doing more angles than usual, it must have taken longer to film. Was there any trouble staying on budget because of his style?

Cheng Pei Pei: Yes, because he's the first one. Always need to have a revolution for that. This film almost burned because Run Run Shaw first saw the movie and he did not agree with a lot of things. At the beginning, I was the only lady in the film. Also I'm half a boy, half a girl. There's never been anything like this before. I did not wear the very pretty traditional Chinese costume. It was very simple. So Run Run didn't think the audience would accept it. So we added a last scene with ten girls there. It was not originally in the script.

Chris: When did you realize you were part of a movie that would change film, being an important part of a martial arts movement?

Cheng Pei Pei: When the audience accepted the film. I recognized we did something different. I had never done a martial arts movie before, and I don't watch those movies. That's like a guy's thing, not me. I loved the musical and love stories. I'm a normal girl.

Chris: There was talk of a *Come Drink with Me* remake with your daughter. What is or was your involvement, and what your thoughts on the possible film?

Cheng Pei Pei: Actually, what I feel is that it should be a musical. My third daughter, Marsha, studied music. I didn't know any musicals until she went to Hong Kong. I just studied to learn about the musical. I think the *Come Drink with Me* story is very simple and would fit with a musical. Right now you see that the story was very complicated, right? You can have something very simple in a martial arts movie, but you look at that and it's actually a very simple one. That's why I think *Come Drink with Me* could always become musical. It's very difficult doing a musical. You need to actually spend more money for that. It was discussed with the company that owns it. I don't think they thought it was a good idea to do at as a musical. We had two completely different ideas for it. One day, I was thinking of doing that film, although maybe not calling it *Come Drink with Me*. I want to memorialize King Hu. That's not the only movie we did together, but it's the first one. I just want to do something for him.

Chris: Are you surprised at all that the movie is still around?

Cheng Pei Pei: I'm not. At that time they didn't have DVD. They only had VHS tape. Because Shaw Brothers never sold any rights, they were copied so many times. When King Hu was still alive, he lived in Pasadena. So we were very close, living a few blocks away from each other. One day, he took me to a Chinese VHS rental place. He told me I should buy that VHS. I don't know if I still have it or not, but it was $35 for a copy. He told me, "You better buy it. Otherwise you will never have a copy." So I bought it. I think it's because the cinema was very wide, but when it comes to the VHS, everyone is very skinny. Because it's a copy of a copy, the color is like black and white. My children watched it before and laughed because they thought it was a black and white movie. The first time Marsha and I went to the Cannes film festival is when Celestial first restored one of my films. Marsha was so surprised that it was in color. The restoration was very good, so it was beautiful. They did a very good job. That's why Shaw Brothers sold their movies to them because now they have DVD. They want to publish to a whole new audience. That's why I say it's not a surprise to me.

Chris: How much of the stunt work did you do yourself for your films?

Cheng Pei Pei: I did most of the stunt work because they didn't like someone doing them for me. They didn't like stunt doubles even though you were doing a stunt. They want you to do it first. Also, I was very young at the time, and I wanted to do it all myself.

Chris: Did you have any complications, such as insurance today, in being able to do your own stunts?

Cheng Pei Pei: We didn't have any insurance. That's very new in Hong Kong.

Chris: You've sustained injuries on films and kept going before this became something that was advertised and talked about. Can you tell me about some of the films you've been injured on and about these experiences?

Cheng Pei Pei: Each one you have some injuries. One of the larger injuries happened when I was riding a horse. You know, the hair is up. I rode below a tree. My hair ends up caught in the tree, but I'm still riding. Also, because I'm using the whip, a guy followed me, and I whip him, you know? The horse was very scared, so he ran very fast. However, my hair is up there and got caught in the tree, so I fell down. At that time, the Shaw Brothers had a bonus for the director if they got it done in time. It's a big deal to them if you are not able to finish the movie because you're hurt. So I just went back to the horse and did it again. Afterwards they took me to the hospital. It was actually hurting a lot. That's why females usually can't do martial arts movies. If you hurt a little bit you might not do it. In this way, I'm very similar with a guy. I never say I'm hurting and can't do it. I always go back to do the shot, so most directors want to use me as their martial arts actress.

On *None But the Brave* (1973) I hurt my ankle on a trampoline. It suddenly became very big. I still needed to finish the film. So they put ice on it to make it numb. That let me finish. Jackie Chan was there. After so many years, I saw him and he said, "We all thought you could never walk anymore." They only knew how to help keep you working. It's not like they had a doctor there. It was very dangerous. I will still feel it sometimes because I didn't take very good care of it at that time. So it's still easy to hurt my ankle. Also, sometimes I would pull my legs too high and hurt my quad. It would come back. Suddenly I can't move my legs. That's a very common injury for a martial arts actress.

Chris: What impact do you believe you had as a female martial arts star?

108

Cheng Pei Pei: Well, we do it every day. During that period of time, I did a lot of martial arts. Every film was a success at the box office. That makes me feel that I really can do martial arts. I feel more interesting doing a martial arts film. In real life, you can rarely be a hero. In a film is the only time I can be a hero.

Chris: Did you ever have females come up and say anything to you in the form of respect?

Cheng Pei Pei: Yes, especially during that period of time. It was very common.

Chris: What were some of those conversations like?

Cheng Pei Pei: Most would say they want to become me. I am an idol of female—stronger and liberal. At that time, women always needed to be a housewife. It made people think in a different way. In real life, I'm just a normal person. I'm still the same. In reality, I'm the mother of four kids!

Chris: Why do you believe the female lead in martial arts movies disappeared, for the most part, until recently?

Cheng Pei Pei: I think it's because before martial arts films were using female, you can't really believe they can fight. Remember how small I am. I'm much smaller than a guy. The audience can't believe me as a hero, right? So, that's why, especially like Bruce Lee, Jackie Chan— more powerful guys came out. The ladies in film just can't do it. They have to be so pretty and sexy. But with something like *Crouching Tiger, Hidden Dragon*, it's a more traditional Chinese story. More females in the lead role have come back, but it's still a lot of guys.

Chris: Did you notice it become difficult to get roles when this decline happened?

Cheng Pei Pei: I think my decline had more to do with age.

Chris: That's when you noticed, when you got older?

Cheng Pei Pei: Yes. I think it's good, though. You have a chance to try different parts. I'm not only doing martial arts movies. I get more variety in my roles.

Chris: Was it intentional playing a lot of your empowered female characters with a quiet dignity?

Cheng Pei Pei: It just happened. I think now, even if I just stand there, they think so. I don't need to try. So that's day by day. It's different with the actress and also I'm very tall compared with most Chinese girls. So with the costumes, it's very easy to fit. Some people need to wear a lot of things to look bigger. That's very different with classical movies and modern movies. Right now, you need to wear less clothes, but that makes you very skinny. Other clothes make you look very big and you seem powerful. That's very important for the fit. They need to have a character fitting. That can make you become that role. That's what King Hu told me. They have a coat and cover your legs. They don't feel you're strong enough to just stand there.

Chris: I noticed a trend in several of your films. It seemed intentional that you didn't have to say anything.

Cheng Pei Pei: Yes, you knew.

Chris: In a lot of films, your characters were the opposite of stereotypical female characters, often very masculine. Did you have any say on this?

Cheng Pei Pei: No. I didn't have any choice.

Chris: Was this ever something you looked for? Did it appeal to you?

Cheng Pei Pei: I think I mostly believe I'm that character. At that time I hadn't married yet. That's why I married at an early age. I became scared. I realized I had become too strong, and no one will want to marry me. For an actor, at some point they can't recognize which is really you and which isn't.

Chris: Did you ever turn down a movie?

Cheng Pei Pei: Yeah, one movie from a Korean director. I didn't like the idea. I refused to do that movie. If I don't like it, I will turn it down. I had more choice at that time. I was able to because I belonged mostly to one company, the Shaw Brothers, and at that time my films were doing good box office. So, at that time, they had the scriptwriter purposefully write it for me. I don't think I would turn anything down that was special for myself. I would talk to the scriptwriter if I didn't feel right, and they'd make it so I felt better.

Chris: In _Lady Hermit_ (1971), your character gives up the man she loves and continues on her journey. What did that ending mean to you and say about your character?

Cheng Pei Pei: I think that relates more to my real life because I wanted to get married. It's more like they want to have another actress come up and become a martial arts movie star—my replacement. To me, I wanted to go to another life.

Chris: Did the passing on the torch work?

Cheng Pei Pei: Later on, she became more successful at being a gamble actress. She did more of those films later on. I don't think anyone can replace anyone. That's what I think. It's very difficult.

Chris: Why was the _Lady Hermit_ advertised as your final screen appearance?

Cheng Pei Pei: Shaw Brothers wanted to do it that way. Because they want to announce more things since I was leaving to get married. When I left, I just left.

Chris: Was your contract up with them?

Cheng Pei Pei: My contract just finished. Yeah, I married. I wanted a very normal life. After they graduate, they marry and have children. That was early 1970s, and normal women always thought that way. I'm just a normal woman.

Chris: What changed to make you return?

Cheng Pei Pei: Actually it's because I divorced. I can't think of anything I can do better than to be an actress. It's easy for me. I tried to do a lot of different things during my marriage. I did real estate and other things. I still love to act. It's still my main interest.

Chris: There was a video company you owned, right?

Cheng Pei Pei: Yeah, I owned a TV production company. I did a lot of different things. Now I'm not, because I want to make more money.

I'm still writing articles for a newspaper, and I'm doing DJ for radio. I just feel I want to do more things not because I can't survive. Now, it's very difficult to survive as an actor. They are always waiting for a job. They don't know when they have work now. Sometimes you can't depend on that. It's very sad to say that, but when I was young, because I belonged to Shaw Brothers, I never needed to worry about it. I had a salary, and I was fine living in a dormitory.

Chris: In *Dragon Swamp* (1969) you got to play dual roles; mother and daughter. What did you try to bring to each role?

Cheng Pei Pei: It was very cute. I was looking for those characters. I try to have very pretty mother and very active daughter to separate two things. It's a very interesting thing. As an actress, we always want to have this kind of opportunity to be two characters.

Chris: You played them both completely different.

Cheng Pei Pei: Yeah.

Chris: What are your thoughts on being called the "Queen of the Swordswomen?"

Cheng Pei Pei: I think my audience and my company gave it to me. They want to say how much they love me.

Chris: Tell me about meeting Ang Lee and the path to being in *Crouching Tiger, Hidden Dragon*.

Cheng Pei Pei: I interviewed him on my talk show. He is very nice. He is a fan of King Hu. He says he wants to do a martial arts movie. I just thought he was kidding. "I'm going to do a martial arts movie. You want to be in it?" I said, "Yeah." Then he said, "How about playing a bad guy?" I never had been a bad guy. Nobody can tell I can be a bad guy, especially a Chinese director. I said, "If you think so, I can try it." When he wanted to do *Crouching Tiger, Hidden Dragon*, only two roles were set. One was me and the other one was Michelle. Then they wanted someone else, the new martial arts actress. He chose a lot of different ones before Ziyi became the lucky one.

Chris: You did another movie with Michelle Yeoh before that, right?

Cheng Pei Pei: Yeah, actually I'm her sifu. I never really shot anything with her. By that time, she was already really famous. I don't know what was wrong with her schedule, but I couldn't wait because I had another movie to do, so they shot my part out first and then shot hers.

Chris: Did you have any idea you were doing yet another film that would have such a large effect on martial arts films?

Cheng Pei Pei: No. That was big surprise. Chow Yun Fat and I always discuss this. Sometimes you shoot with a director and you know. You know what it will turn out like, but with this movie we never guessed. We were very surprised it became so huge. If you have the right timing and everything is perfect, then something will happen.

Chris: Tell me about working with Stephen Chow.

Cheng Pei Pei: At first it was going to be a movie with Stephen and Gong Li. I never understand his movies. I'm not into his comedy. I don't have that kind of humor. When I returned from my agent, she said, "Stephen Chow is very famous now. You better be in his movie. People will notice you're coming back." I said, "I don't understand his movie." Why doesn't an actress understand? So I rented all his movies and then watched them and tried to understand. I told my agent I think I can do it. I got it because Gong Li just won award and didn't want to do it. Most of what you see of me was for her, not me. We were shooting at six o'clock in the morning, and she was very tired and didn't want to do it. Stephen Chow was pretty gentle and didn't want to push her too much. You can't do comedy by yourself. You need to have partner. So that's why Stephen Chow came to me and asked me if I wanted to do it. My part got bigger and bigger. I learned to do serious comedy from him. He is very serious. Normal life is very quiet. I still don't understand his films. I don't like *Kung Fu Hustle* (2004) very much, but I like *CJ7* (2008). I think a lot of things he's repeating. It's very difficult to have something new. He tries very hard. With *CJ7*, he had more drama, and I loved it.

Chris: Sammo Hung.

Cheng Pei Pei: He is very hard working. When I first met him, he was just a little boy. He's about five or six years younger than me. He always works very hard. He has very good film sense. Not everyone understands. Even though he's very fat, very big, he works very hard.

Chris: Chow Yun Fat.

Cheng Pei Pei: I love him. He is a superstar. He says that I'm a superstar. He's lovely. He loves my family. All my children love him.

Chris: What are your thoughts on the current state of martial arts films?

Cheng Pei Pei: I think it's become more difficult in the international market because people have seen that movie. They want more. I think the good martial arts movies still need the base of a very good story. The fighting is nothing. Especially now, the techniques are very easy. You can use a computer for all the things. The story, the characters are the most important.

Chris: What types of roles are you looking for today?

Cheng Pei Pei: All kinds. I'm interested in different things. I'm getting older. I think as an actress, if I can play all kinds of different roles, it's a little more interesting. I think I'm very lucky to still have a lot of different roles I can play because of my life experience.

BRIDGETT "BABY DOLL"
RILEY

LIKE OTHER MARTIAL ARTIST INTERVIEWEES, BRIDGETT "BABY DOLL" Riley got her start while training as a gymnast. Watching her brother Patrick compete, Bridgett switched sports to karate in a move that would alter her life forever. Since she began studying karate, Bridgett has won over 300 trophies and earned a 5th degree black belt. Karate would lead to kickboxing. Bridgett boldly got herself the opportunity to train at the legendary Jet Center. Bridgett would win five titles in three separate weight divisions. Later, Bridgett would transition yet again to boxing. She would win the IFBA bantamweight championship. Although she costarred alongside Dale "Apollo" Cook and Ron Hall in *Triple Impact* (1992), it was her stunt work that has created yet another career. Bridgett

Photo courtesy of Bridgett Riley.

"Baby Doll" Riley has performed stunts in such films as *Iron Man 2* (2010), *The Hangover* (2009), *Million Dollar Baby* (2004), and numerous others.

Notable roles
Triple Impact
Million Dollar Baby
Iron Man 2
Bare Knuckles

Chris: What were you like as a child?

Bridgett: I was very introverted. I was really, really shy. I had big, thick glasses. I went to Catholic school, so I didn't know how to dress. I was kind of a geek. I was not shy around my family, though. That's when I was a little knucklehead.

Chris: Does anything come to mind from your childhood that helped you in martial arts training?

Bridgett: I had an awesome family life, so I was very close to my brothers and parents. My younger brother was the karate kid. I was the gymnast. I think the gymnastics definitely helped me. Once I started studying karate, I came out of my shell. I got contacts and things began to change.

Chris: What inspired you to begin training in martial arts?

Bridgett: My brother Patrick completely inspired me. He's my hero to this day. I'm such a fan of my brother. I was so nervous to take my first karate class. I watched three classes, and they kept asking me, "Why don't you jump in?" I kept saying, "I'm going to watch one more." I was terrified. Once I did it, I was begging, "Can I spar?" It was weird. I was home. This is where it's at. I begged to spar and, eventually, they let me. It was very cool. I focused on it, trying to get as good as I can. I was obsessed. My brother and I were there seven days a week. They couldn't get rid of us. I loved the camaraderie of working with my brother.

Chris: What influence did your parents have on your interest in martial arts?

Bridgett: My mom and dad influenced me in such a positive way because they drove us. They took us to karate every single night. They were involved. They went to every single karate tournament. They were big, supportive fans. They loved it. It was their social life too. We would travel regionally. Back then, we didn't have a lot of money to get on the national circuit. They would invite different teams over to spend the night at our house. My mom and dad were so awesome. I couldn't have had more support in my sports.

Chris: What was your friends and family's reaction to you studying martial arts?

Bridgett: My family loved me learning martial arts. They were a little concerned about me stopping gymnastics because I had dreams of going to the Olympics. It was a huge decision. I just said, "Mom, I want to stop gymnastics." I don't like to call it quitting, because I was transferring it to another journey. My mom said, "Okay, if this is what you really want." They completely supported me.

I didn't have a whole lot of friends. I was always kind of a one best friend person. I wasn't social. I'm still a loner. They thought it was cool, though. Especially when I got my black belt, everyone's saying, "She's a bad ass. Put her in front!" You know how people are. I had to tell them, "I don't fight on the streets. I just fight in karate tournaments. This is sports." Everybody seemed excited about it.

Chris: Before you started training in martial arts, what was your impression?

Bridgett: I just had a little knowledge of karate from my brother being involved. I have to think back. We all went to my gymnastic meets, and we all went to Patrick's karate tournaments. That was my introduction to karate. I was fascinated, especially when I saw the

118

girls. It was a trip because I was thinking, "I can do that." Something went on fire inside of me. It was really cool. I think it's going to be very difficult to parallel that type of passion for something else. Even to this day, I'm looking for that same type of thing because it was overwhelming. I remember feeling that I had to do it.

Chris: When you were starting out, did it feel natural?

Bridgett: I had to practice a ton, but I felt like I was home. I was a complete natural. I didn't have to think about it. I had no fear. It was amazing because toward the end of my gymnastic career, I started to get fear. I had a couple of falls, and it was getting so hard. I had some blocks, but I didn't in martial arts.

Chris: How did you become interested in kickboxing?

Bridgett: Kickboxing piggybacked off my karate endeavors. I earned my black belt in Missouri and acquired a bit of success for several years on the regional karate tournament circuit alongside my brother Patrick. I know that for me, traditional martial arts have been the foundation in which all of my fighting success has stemmed from. Not to mention some of my favorite memories have been etched in my life up to this point through the martial arts. Karate point fighting pointed out, pun intended, the discovery that I really like to *keep* hitting – especially *after* the break. We dabbled in continuous point fighting, but it still was not scratching my itch that began to grow fiercely. Finally, my first kickboxing instructor out of Belleville, Illinois, Jim Boucher, suggested I try my hand at a professional kickboxing match. An amateur fight was a nice "idea" in theory, but the reality back then was that if I were to fight, I'd go pro right off the bat. I had no other thought, but "Heck yeah," and "Bring it!" So we did. My first fight was a victory against the U.S. Champion. I was hooked.

Chris: What led you to the Jet Center?

Bridgett: I lost a fight. I was green like broccoli. I didn't know any better until I tasted defeat. It broke my heart in a way that I can compare

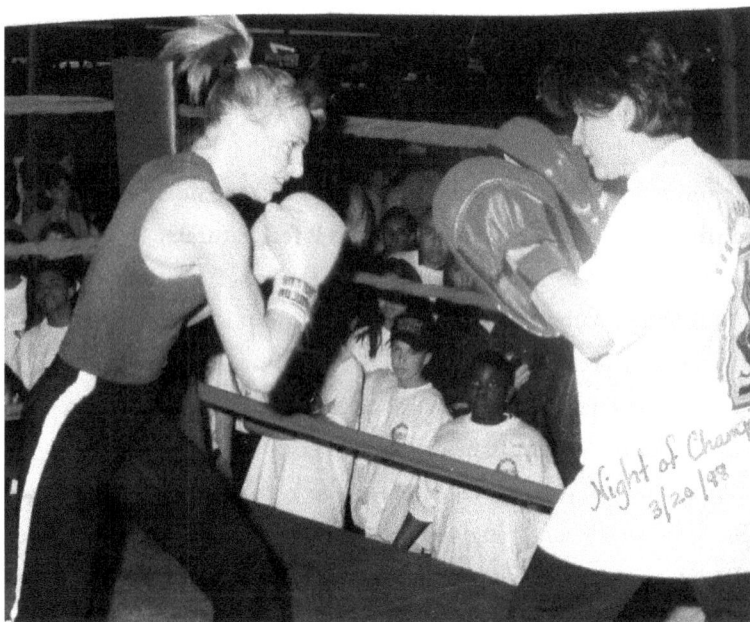

Bridgett with Lilly. Photo courtesy of Bridgett Riley.

nothing to. I was determined, with the help of my late father Chuck and my brother Patrick, to move to L.A. as quickly as I could. What *then* I considered to be a "failure," was actually *the* turning point in my life. This event drove me passionately to the San Fernando Valley with a c-note to my name, a beat up car, and a little bit of raw talent in desperate need of development. I landed in the right spot; The World Famous Jet Center, the original. I met her. She would become my mentor and trainer/manager alongside her husband "Blinky" Rodriguez. Her being the late Mrs. Lilly Urquidez Rodriguez. She saw something in me. I won the lottery when she said, "Bridgett, if you're serious, move here, dedicate your *all* to this sport, and we will take you on as one of our fighters." Epic!

Chris: Tell me about training with Lilly and Benny.

Bridgett: I was around Benny, "Blinky," Peter Cunningham, and several other great fighters. It was a dream made real to be included among this level of talent. Lilly was my biggest inspiration. She and I had a unique bond. She put everything into me. Lilly went above and beyond, in many ways, to instill in me the importance of becoming not only a world class athlete but also becoming a world class person. She guided me closer to Christ, which is the most important relationship I have in my life. Lil taught me about sacrifice, dedication, and a work ethic in the gym that is priceless. My life was running and training. My social life took a back seat to my desire to become a world champion.

Chris: When do you believe someone should start studying martial arts?

Bridgett: I believe anyone can start martial arts at any time. That's what I love about martial arts. There might be a minimum, like five or six, but you can do this until the day you die. That's what so awesome about the martial arts. You never stop learning.

Chris: Give me an idea about your training.

Bridgett: Back when I was starting, we were in the dojo seven days a week. We were obsessed. It was school and then karate. We lived there in the summers. I couldn't get enough of it. I really worked on my form. I'm such a perfectionist that I'm really a technician. Also, I couldn't spar enough—that was just fun. Sparring my brother was the most fun. We loved each other so much, but he would light a fire in me. When we were sparring, I'd just want to kill him.

Chris: How has your training changed today?

Bridgett: Today, I'm retired from professional fighting, but I'm working as an actress and stuntwoman. I train when I can. I definitely miss being in the gym. Right now, I really love being in the boxing gym. I want to stay sharp, and I am by nature a gym rat. I love the boxing workout. Working hard is part of my DNA, but it's not at the intensity it was when I was actively fighting as my profession. I kick with a team of stunt people on occasion to keep what I have. Running is a form of therapy for me and how I keep my weight

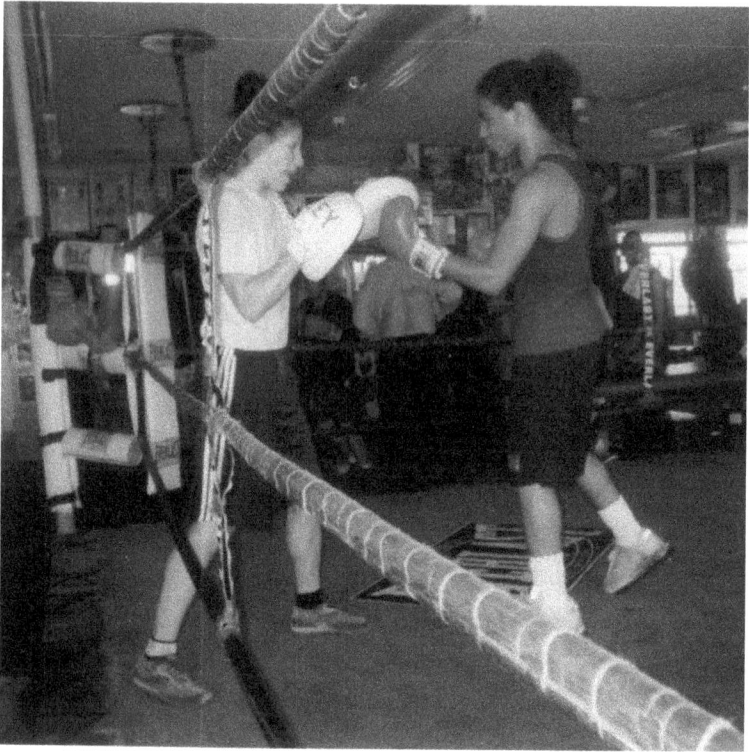

Bridgett training with Corbin Bleu.
Photo courtesy of Bridgett Riley.

down when doubling skinny actresses. More importantly, it's where I get to think and touch nature. Living in Los Angeles lends incredible places to hike, run, and tackle cross country journeys. I am currently training at an intense acting studio. This is my new challenge, my new world title, if you will, I am going after. I am blessed to work as a professional stuntwoman, and I would love to monkey bar into more acting. I enjoy teaching and training in between gigs. I work with actors for film and television, and that is a lot of fun for me. Working with Angelina Jolie in Los Angeles for a few weeks while she was on vacation was a highlight for me. I assisted and worked diligently with Malin Ackerman on *Watchmen* (2009) and doubled her. There are several awesome actresses I've been able to train and work with in this incredible business. I pinch myself still at times and pray for safety and excellence.

Chris: What sort of training would you suggest to someone just starting out?

Bridgett: I would suggest they train at least three days a week. You have to put the time in. It's so easy to forget what you learn. Any martial art requires a lot of repetition, consistency, dedication, and persistence. You have to stick to it. Don't just join the first dojo you see. You really have to watch the instructors, check out all the classes, look at the students, and research online.

Chris: What advice would you give to a beginning female kickboxer?

Bridgett: Find a good gym. Find a good trainer. Train hard. Cut *no* corners, for there are *no* short cuts if you choose to obtain longevity. Commit to the work. It is a process that takes time. Grasp this concept, it is your friend. Surround yourself with good people with good motives. Go to the gym to work, it's not social hour. Get in and get out. Rest hard. Eat right. Keep on keeping on, and when you feel like giving up—*don't!* That's where you begin. This is the place where you grow. Don't miss it.

Chris: Your workouts and training have a lot of physical requirements. How would you describe your diet?

Bridgett: I'm a foodie. I love gourmet food and wine. I love pairing food with wine. However, I also have to double these skinny, anorexic actresses, which really puts a cramp on my eating. I try to do a lot of lean proteins. I love meat, though. I'm definitely not a vegan or vegetarian. I am trying to do more salads. I love fish. I love really good protein bars. My favorite cheat food is pizza. I don't neglect the good stuff. I just try to reward myself about once a week. I try to cut the carbs because I'm trying to stay lean. It's hard because I have so much muscle. It's very difficult for me to lose muscle, but a lot of these actresses have no muscle. I get told constantly that I'm too muscular. It's a constant battle for me. Several producers have told me I'm too thick and have to lose weight. That is the reality of the business. I need to be a 2, but I'm a 4. I'm working on it.

Chris: What do you feel are the most important attributes of a successful martial artist?

Bridgett: You have to have the desire. You have to be surrounded by knowledgeable, good people who know what they're doing and have your best interests at heart. You have to have dedication. It's okay to have fear. I had fear every time you walk in the ring, but it's what you do with it. Have the fear but continue to move forward. Don't let it stop you. Don't be worried about what other people think. That can stop a lot of people. I think martial arts is very personal. I think it's a personal journey. It's hard not to compare yourself to other people. I really want to stress, especially to young girls, don't worry about how well you're doing. It's really about you. Stay focused on your process and how well you're doing at getting it.

Chris: If someone is studying a martial art but is not focused and disciplined, what advice would you give them to make changes?

Bridgett: Think about a new hobby. You have to be focused. If you're not there, you're just wasting your own time. It's not serving them.

Chris: How did you know you were ready to step into the ring the first time?

Bridgett: Unless you're a knucklehead like me, I believe your instructor should tell you. You should have some basics. It's good to have that. I cannot stress enough that we never have our basics good enough. Not even the masters. Basics are the foundation, and you can't do enough repetition on that. Have good gear. I suggest going to a dentist to have a very good mouthpiece made. Just go for it after asking your instructor.

Chris: What was your first karate competition like?

Bridgett: I was so nervous. I had to talk myself into it. I had to play mental games with myself. I had to do that in kickboxing and boxing too. I was so excited. I loved the sparring the most. It's weird because you're so nervous, but as soon as they say, "Fight," it goes away. You are in it, and it's so exciting. I loved it.

Chris: When you were in a competition, can you think of a time where you had to change your fighting style for an opponent?

Bridgett: I had to adjust to different styles. The most unorthodox would throw me through a loop. The cleaner the fighter was, the better I was. The sloppy ones, the ones that came out like gangbusters or an octopus were difficult. I had to learn how to deal with that. I had to learn how to stuff them. I had to learn timing. I had to learn it's better to come off first sometimes and other times it's better to counter. You don't have a lot of time to figure that out. In kickboxing, I can take a couple and figure it out. I was glad to have my background because you have to be quick. You have to make adjustments quick. You have to adjust all the time for different fighters and styles.

Chris: Who would you say was your toughest opponent?

Bridgett: Christine Bannon. It was difficult to get past her sidekick. She was very flexible. I didn't get an opportunity to go to a lot of nationals. That's when I made the decision to jump into kickboxing. I did everything within my means and area while doing karate, so the decision made sense. Later, we worked together. She's a good person. I think she's really cool.

Chris: At any point do you feel like you became a role model for females?

Bridgett: I believe I have. I've gotten a lot of feedback from young kids. Even from boys. I know I was a role model as a martial artist. I think it grew as I pursued other things.

Chris: If a female were entering a competition today and wanted your advice, what would you tell her?

Bridgett: I would tell her to just go out there and go for it. Do the best you can. Don't over or under estimate who you're up against. Go in there hungry. Go in there as if it's me or them. Use your skills.

Photo courtesy of Bridgett Riley.

Try not to put too much pressure on yourself. Try to have a good time. Try to remember you love this. When it becomes a job, you lose the beauty and joy of why we're doing this.

Chris: Do you feel satisfied with your competitive career?

Bridgett: I'm extremely satisfied with my competitive career. I would have loved to be on a national circuit with a team. That was a dream of mine, but I don't regret anything. I loved that I jumped right into kickboxing. I couldn't have had a better career. I feel very blessed. It was an incredible ride. I accomplished a lot of goals and dreams. When my dad was alive, he was the one who wanted me on the cover of *Black Belt Magazine*. He would show me pictures of Kathy Long and say, "That's got to be you." I accomplished world titles in both boxing and kickboxing. I'm very pleased.

Chris: How did you get involved with *Triple Impact* (1992)?

Bridgett: Oh my gosh, that was Dale "Apollo" Cook, and I was fighting in Missouri. I started fighting for Dale "Apollo" Cook, and he approached me with, "I have an opportunity for you." I told him I'm a fighter and not an actress. I was thinking, "I'm not going to do that!" He was saying, "Think about it. It's in Manila. It's some money. You'll have a lot of fun." I was so young. We went over there, and I had the time of my life.

Chris: What are Dale Cook and Ron Hall like to work with?

Bridgett: They were awesome and very supportive. They would rehearse when I needed it. They were fun and positive. I didn't know anything, though. If I could put that one under the rug, I'd be good. It's all about experiences.

Chris: Describe a typical preparation for a fight scene.

Bridgett: You hope you have a really good fight choreographer. I really like when you have someone good. They watch you and see what you can do. They try it out and see what you can do. They are not stuck in one style. They make it work. There's a lot of practice and working on it. I like repetition. I'm a very hard worker. When we first start, I may not have it. But once I've got it, it'll be good. I look in mirrors a lot. I'll go home and think about it. Once I have it, we can shoot it.

Chris: What would you consider to be your best fight scene?

Bridgett: A fight scene that got cut up on *Serenity* (2005). I was working with the best guys. Their reactions sold what I did, but it was better in rehearsals. It's on my demo reel. I love the fight. I liked my rehearsal from *Serenity*.

Chris: How often does that happen where a rehearsal is great but the final product is not?

Bridgett: That happens often. A lot of people don't know how to shoot action. You can have the best fight in the world, but if it's shot wrong, it's going to look like crap. It'll be dull, flat, and boring. You can take a bad fight and make it look great. There's an art to shooting action. It's how they shoot it. It can look completely different than how it was rehearsed. There are so many factors in that.

Chris: What would you consider to be your most difficult stunt?

Bridgett: I just did stair fall without a lot of padding. I was very nervous about it. It was gnarly. I've done a lot of tricky wire stuff. It almost knocks you out.

Chris: How did you get involved in being a stuntwoman?

Bridgett: I morphed into the biz by being at the right place at the right time. An entertainment manager was watching me train at the Jet Center and approached me. He told me I should go in and read for a part that seemed written for me. I found myself in a room with about twelve Asian ladies. "Hmmmm," I'm thinking. I read. They had already cast Amy Jo Johnson for the Pink Ranger. The people in charge made a spot for me anyway. That was cool with me. My first gig was an acting one on the television series *The Mighty Morphin Power Rangers*. I played a small part as a character called Sharky. It was an experience. I watched the Japanese stunt team rehearsing and envied the stuff they got to do. Later, a pal suggested to the coordinator that he audition me, and I was hired as a stuntwoman.

This job opened up the stunt world to me, and I received it. This is when I juggled stunts with professional fighting. My passion and heart were in the fight game, but the stunt work paid the bills.

Chris: What are your plans for the future?

Bridgett: I just did a movie with Martin Kove. I want to continue doing more stunt work. I'm very open. I want to stay positive. I want to be the best example and role model to others. I have a heart for people who have been in abusive relationships. I have been in one. I'd like to help girls in that position. Even being a world champion, I've been there. I would love the opportunity to do more speaking or whatever.

I'm taking things one day at a time. I am married now to my high school crush! Acting is *big* on my list of learning and experiencing it on a serious level raises the bar for me. Ultimately it is up to God. I pray for his will and his direction. God helps those who help themselves and, of course, others along the way. So in the meantime, I want to train, work, play, and enjoy every moment of life and see where the ride takes me.

Photo courtesy of Cynthia Rothrock.

CYNTHIA
ROTHROCK

AT THIRTEEN, CYNTHIA ROTHROCK BEGAN TAKING MARTIAL ARTS lessons. Unbeknownst to anyone at the time, Cynthia would alter the martial arts world for generations of women. Cynthia quickly became one of the best at Kata and weapons, challenging both males and females in competitions. For four years, she was the World Karate Champion in forms and weapons competition. Cynthia won five black belts, hundreds of tournament and competitions wins, hundreds of trophies, multiple hall of fame inductions, and numerous other accolades.

Outside of the martial arts world, Cynthia Rothrock is known as an action hero. Cynthia was paired up with Michelle Yeoh in *Yes, Madam* (1985), launching both women into stardom. Cynthia again broke barriers, but this time in film, by being a white female who found success as a heroine in a male-dominated Asian film business. She would take on Sammo Hung in a classic fight scene for *Shanghai Express* (1986) and get a starring role in *Blonde Fury* (1989). The Hong Kong films include impressive fight scenes that would make Rothrock a worldwide star. She was able to achieve memorable moves that had rarely, and in some cases never, been seen before.

The home video business was booming worldwide, and Cynthia was given the chance to headline numerous films in America. Cynthia was the lead in the *China O'Brien* and *Lady Dragon* franchises. She would be teamed-up in numerous other franchises, such as *Rage and Honor* and *Martial Law*. Her film popularity can be seen in the large number of sequels she made in a time when it wasn't a fad. While the films proved popular, they did not contain the memorable action scenes of her earlier work. The 2000s have been mostly comprised of team-ups with other video boom stars, like Don "The Dragon" Wilson and her frequent costar Richard Norton. Cynthia remains a fan favorite, frequently appearing at conventions and shows worldwide.

Notable roles
Yes, Madam
Blonde Fury
Lady Dragon
Rage and Honor

Chris: How did your childhood differ from a typical one?
Cynthia: I don't think it differed so much. My dad was around a lot more than my mom because she managed a store. When I was little, she was only around on weekends. I was a daddy's little girl but that's common. I grew up fishing and him teaching me how to swim by throwing me in the water. The career I went into it made sense because I grew up as a tough little kid.

Chris: Were you very athletic growing up?

Cynthia: I was, but I wasn't involved in sports in school. I liked to climb trees and fences. I would go on scary rides on amusement parks. It's funny because I never did sports in school. My daughter is in school, and I'm looking at sports thinking, "Why didn't I do that?" As far as being active, I was very physical. I started doing martial arts at a young age, so that took over when I got older. I guess that took all my focus.

Chris: What drew you to start practicing martial arts?

Cynthia: I was a young teen. I did a lot of things. I did baton, dancing, guitar, and a lot of things that I didn't stick with. I had a friend whose parents were studying martial arts. I watched them practice, giving me my first look at seeing martial arts. I thought I wanted to try it. Being that young, I thought the uniforms were cute. How cool would it be to earn a belt? Seeing them practice made me think that I wanted to try it. When I first tried it, I hated it and wanted to quit. My mom wouldn't let me because she was so fed up with me starting things and not finishing. She said, "I signed you up for four months. You are going to continue." During that four months time, my instructor gave a speech to everyone that if you're not good, it's because you're not practicing. I thought he was looking at me. I got embarrassed and thought, "I don't practice." I had another month and a half on my contract so I started practicing. Within two weeks, everything that I was afraid to attempt and try and didn't like came very easy to me. That was a good lesson for me. If you're not good at something, don't give up. You can be, but you need to put some work and effort toward it. I started getting good, and I loved it.

Chris: From the time you first started in martial arts until now, when you're teaching it, did you see an increase in the number of females that participate?

Cynthia: Oh, definitely. When I first started, there was only one other lady in the class. It was never that big. When I got my black belt, there might have been five or six. At that time, it was considered a man's sport. I would go to Alaska and do a seminar. I remember people saying, "Oh, you train in martial arts?" I'm going, "Yeah, why not?" I think there was a big fallacy at the time, that you had to be big and strong or you couldn't be effective in martial arts. I think as the years went by, people realized it wasn't a man's sport, and it's actually appealing for someone to be able to defend themselves instead of hiding. Also, the idea of knowing how to defend yourself is something everyone wants to know. The years went by and people started seeing more martial arts and women out there. It keeps increasing yearly, so there's a huge difference between now and then. When I used to compete, I was in women's divisions that were white and black belts. I wouldn't think about it. In my first tournament I took second against the black belts. Now it's so easy in competition because you have lightweight, heavyweight, karate, and kung fu. I never had that luxury. There just weren't that many women. When I competed in weapons, in the mid-'80s, I had to compete against the men. That was the first time a woman, according to the national rankings, had ever taken the title competing in men's.

Chris: What was the best training advice you received when you were starting out?

Cynthia: I think what I mentioned before about how if you're not good it's your own self. You're being lazy and not putting your mind to it. You're defeating yourself before you even try. I think the best advice is that you're going to get what you put into it. If you put 100 percent, you'll get 100 percent out. Do not attempt something with a negative attitude. "Oh, I can't do this. I don't have enough power. I'm the only girl." You can't come in with a defeatist attitude. You have to go into it positive, set your goals, and work toward it.

Chris: Demonstrating self-defense has become an integral part of your life. Do you believe you're respected more for self-defense because you're a female?

Cynthia: Back then, definitely. Just from competition, and when I first started doing the movies, people started seeing me. They'd see me and say, "If you can do it, I can do it." I'm five foot three. I'm not a big person. They would say, "Could you be a lawyer in your next movie? You're just a good role model for us." I think it is all that fallacy that you have to be big and strong in order to be effective. Even today, people will say, "You're the reason I started martial arts." One time a producer I had just met said, "You are the role model for my four-year-old daughter." That made me feel really good. If women or girls can look up and say, "I want to do that. I want to be like her." It's all positive and good. At the same time, I'm an advocate that all women should know self-defense. The more time goes on, the more you have to know it. I don't think the world was as scary in the eighties as it is now.

Chris: A couple of women I interviewed told me how they were abused. What do you think is the best strategy for women to defend themselves in this situation?

Cynthia: First of all, nobody should take abuse. If you don't know how to defend yourself, then you're going to go to the police. That's your strongpoint. If you know how to defend yourself, no matter who it is—a husband, neighbor, or someone you don't know—you're going to defend yourself and then call the police. I would assume that if someone's in a position where they're getting abused or raped, they go out and learn self-defense so it won't happen again. It's a shame that someone has to let something like that happen before they start seeking how to defend themselves. That's why I think everyone should know how to defend themselves. I've heard that many times when doing self-defense classes for women. A lot of those women have been abused or attacked and they say, "I'm not going to put myself in that position again. I'm going to learn how to defend myself."

Chris: Have you ever been forced to use your skills in self-defense?

Cynthia: No. It's interesting because a lot of people I know haven't. I have been in situations where I may have had to use it. When you are confident with yourself and know how to defend yourself, you are aware of situations. If I park somewhere and it's late, I'm looking around and staying aware. I have my keys in my hand that I could use. I'm very aware. By training, you're aware of your surroundings. I remember being in New Orleans, and there was an event going on. My friend and I were the only Caucasian people walking on the street. People were trying to intimidate us. I was like, "You're not going to scare me." You have a confidence in yourself. People will prey on weak people. They won't mess with someone who's confident. They want someone who looks afraid.

Chris: How did you get started in Hong Kong cinema?

Cynthia: At that point, I was number one in foreign weapons, and I was on the West Coast demonstration team with Ernie Reyes. He had a call from the editor of *Inside Kung Fu* at the time, saying there was a Hong Kong company that was coming to Los Angeles and having auditions because they wanted to look for a new, Caucasian Bruce Lee. They were trying to build somebody up for that. Ernie said, "Can we bring this girl?" They said I could come, but they weren't looking for girls. We went down to a school. We all did some things, and I did some form, weapons, fought, and some self-defense. They decided to go with me instead of a guy. That's how I got started. They didn't use me. Two years went by so I thought, "I'm never going to do a film. That company has forgotten about me." Then I did a piece for Peter Jennings on *World News Tonight*. Someone had seen an article about me in a San Francisco newspaper, so Peter Jennings called me to do a news clip on me. They said in the story that I had a contract with a Hong Kong company, but they never used me. They ended it by saying, "Look out Hong Kong, here she comes!" Sammo Hung saw it in Hong Kong and said, "Who's this girl?" That's how I got started in Hong Kong is through them seeing the story on Peter Jennings. They called me, and within three or four months I was off to Hong Kong to shoot *Yes, Madam.*

Chris: What do you consider to be the greatest part of the Hong Kong cinema experience?

Cynthia: The greatest experience is working with geniuses of choreography. To this day, my mind is still blown away that I did the things they had me do. The choreography is just brilliant. It was really tough. I actually thought I was going to get killed if I stayed over there doing films. The opportunity to work with these geniuses and doing the films that I did was probably my greatest memory of Hong Kong movies.

Chris: Did you feel you had to earn respect more for being a Caucasian or female?

Cynthia: Interesting point. At that time, there weren't that many women. There was Angela Mao from the early Bruce Lee movies. It wasn't a popular thing. The only time they used Caucasians in Hong Kong was as the bad guys. I don't think they ever had someone, at that point, star. With *Yes, Madam,* they wanted to do this movie and use Michelle Yeoh and this American girl. When I went there, I earned respect on the first night. From that point on, everybody really respected me. It was this move that was really, really hard to do. I had to kick one of the stunt guys, and he grabbed my foot. At the same time, I had to jump up, spin around and kick him with my other foot. It was the leg I couldn't kick with too. Everybody has a side that is better. I couldn't get it. I was thinking, "Oh my God, they're going to think I stink." I finally figured it out because nobody could speak English to me. Everybody spoke Cantonese. When I did it, I did it so good that I jumped up and kicked the stuntman in the face. Then I was all petrified that I hurt him, but everyone was so amazed on the set that I did that. I kept trying and trying, and never said "I can't do this." They all started clapping. From that point on, I never felt that they didn't respect me because I gave 110 percent and did things that the average person wouldn't want to do. I just tried whatever they told me, and I did my best. I never felt that because I was a woman or Caucasian that were any prejudices against me there.

Chris: How did the "Rothrock Sting" develop?

Cynthia: That's a funny thing. It developed when I was doing demonstrations with the West Coast demonstration team. George Cheung and I used to do all these demonstrations, and I would try to come up with the craziest and funniest moves that we could do. At that point, I was number one in forms so I was doing gymnastics and ballet classes. I would do anything I could to improve my martial arts. While I was in a ballet class, they had us on the bar and said, "Kick your leg." I did and hit myself in the head. I went, "Oh, man that hurts." I went to George and said, "Grab me in a headlock and let me see if I can kick you in the head." I did it and almost knocked him out. I was blown away that it worked, and it became a part of our demonstrations. That's how it developed. I never named it, but people gave it that name. That's how it developed, though.

Chris: I'm going to list off some names and want you to comment on them. First, Michelle Yeoh.

Cynthia: Michelle Yeoh was actually my friend. She was probably my savior in Hong Kong because I didn't know anyone. She spoke English and was a girl who I could hang out with. She made that first eight months of the shooting much easier for me.

Chris: Sammo Hung.

Cynthia: Sammo Hung is such a genius that when I did that fight scene with him, everyone was scared for me because he hits hard. He's so big. He did hit hard and he was big, but he was very gentle at the same time. His brilliance is what I remember about him.

Chris: Corey Yuen.

Cynthia: Corey Yuen is my favorite director in the entire world who I've worked with. I loved working with him. I thought we had a very good connection. We could understand what was going on. He was funny. He tested me beyond what I thought I could do. He's my favorite of all the people I met in Hong Kong.

Chris: David Carradine.

Cynthia: David was a good friend of mine. I knew him more as a friend than a martial artist. We had a good, mutual friend. David was a very intellectual, smart guy. He was a good friend.

Chris: What differences do you find between being in a fight scene with a male or female?

Cynthia: I can fight a little tougher with a male. I can hit them harder and not worry about it. When I was fighting Karen Sheperd in *Yes, Madam*, Corey Yuen kept whispering "You've got to stop fighting so hard or she's going to go home." I was used to fighting all the stuntmen.

Chris: Tell me about your fight scenes with the following. First, Bolo Yeung.

Cynthia: I was surprised with that one. With Bolo coming from Hong Kong, I thought he'd be like a Hong Kong stuntman, but he didn't want to get hit. He wanted to make it like you almost hit someone, but you don't really do it. I was expecting him to be like a stuntman and not an actor.

Chris: Karen Sheperd.

Cynthia: Karen is a trooper. She came to Hong Kong. At that time, we weren't friends, but we are now. Corey Yuen said to me, "We're looking for a woman to fight you that could do the steel whip." He named a couple of people. I said, "We're not really friends, but I think Karen is the best that could do it." During that film, we became friends. A situation happened where she was getting frustrated and couldn't get the move. She walked off the set and was a little sad. I went to her and said, "You know what? Don't worry about it. Just say you can't do it. Change the move." She came back and everything was fine. I think shooting a movie in Hong Kong bonded our friendship.

Before, we didn't really know each other, but now she's my friend today. I respect her. She was the forms competitor before I was, so she was the dominant in the field. She was very good.

Chris: Richard Norton.

Cynthia: Richard is one of my best friends in martial arts. We've done close to fifteen movies together. We're trying to get two scripts made now. I think out of all the relationships I've had in martial arts with people, Richard has remained one of my really good friends way back from the second movie I ever did. We still want to do movies together. It's rare when you meet someone on a set. Usually you are friends, but when the movie finishes you end up going your own ways. You don't see them, but Richard and I have kept in touch all these years. If he had a project, he'll recommend me and vice versa. That relationship will go on forever.

Fight scenes are always easier when you know someone. I met him on *Millionaire's Express*. You end up hanging out together, and you can talk about the scene. You can talk about how hard to hit, and what we want to do. It's much easier.

Chris: What do you think makes an interesting fight scene?

Cynthia: I think good choreography is number one. Number two is having a good stuntperson. A lot of people think that if a stuntperson isn't good then you're not going to look good. I always say to people when I'm doing choreography at a seminar, "Your role is so important because if you don't react or you're not strong, that star is not going to look good."

Chris: Do you prefer the long preparation of the Hong Kong fight scene or the quick American way?

Cynthia: Strangely enough, I like the hard one. I haven't had the luxury of being on a big American film. I've only been on films that shoot on an average of like three or five weeks. I much prefer the time, rehearsals, and coverage of a Hong Kong film. Sometimes, when you're doing an American film, especially a small budget, you might only have forty-five minutes to do a fight scene. You're comparing a fight scene that might be eight days in Hong Kong, so there's going to be a major difference in what your fight scene looks like. I prefer the Hong Kong fighting.

Chris: In *Yes, Madam*, there's a scene where you do the splits on the wall while using a staff to fight off the villains.

Cynthia: I didn't do anything to prepare for that one. They talked about it, saying "We're going to put this teeny ledge on the wall and you're going to do a split against it. What we're going to do is have you on that little ledge. Your leg is going to be hanging over your head and we're going to put a wire over your waist so you snap against the wall into a split." I did it and had no problem doing it. The problem is that they kept me there for three hours. They said, "Can you stay there? Are you comfortable?" I was like, "Oh yeah." After three hours, because it was such a big rig, I didn't walk for four days because my legs were so sore.

Steve Carver directs David Carradine in *Lone Wolf McQuade* (1983).
Photo courtesy of Steve Carver.

Chris: There was a movie you were attached to titled *Split Lightning*. It was written by Courtney Joyner and was supposed to costar David Carradine and have a Chuck Norris cameo. Could you tell me about that project?

Cynthia: It was a movie by Steve Carver. There were problems between the producers and the movie. I think some sort of personal relationship went off the road and the project died.

Chris: Is it true that part of the agreement was that you would change your image and look?

Cynthia: No, it was a disagreement between the people behind the scenes. It wasn't about me. I'd be okay with that. My hair color is always changing. I think they had a financial deal that didn't go right and there were lawsuits involved. Steve Carver got disillusioned with the entertainment industry and walked away. Whenever I would see him years later, he wasn't doing films anymore. I think it might have started with that. You trust people and think they're your friends and then they turn around and try to sue you. You kind of go, "I don't like this industry."

Chris: Does it bother you to do a movie like *Redemption* where you do one trademark kick and then you're killed off?

Cynthia: No, it doesn't bother me because it's a job. I'm an actress looking for jobs. Would I have liked to have a bigger part or fight scene? Definitely, but that's not what I was hired to do. I was hired to do that role. I would say it didn't bother me because I knew what it called for before I agreed to do it.

Chris: In *Blonde Fury*, you use high heels to your advantage in a fight scene. In *Manhattan Chase* (2000), you use a purse. Do you feel using these feminine objects adds another layer to the films?

Cynthia: Definitely. That's the thing I love about Hong Kong is the creativity. That scene with the high heels is one that I look at and go, "Wow! Was that really me?" Would you tell a class to train in high heels? No, but for pure entertainment. As for the purse, when

142

I first started doing kung fu in New York, I would drive to train. Afterwards, we would go out to Chinatown to watch some Hong Kong movies. That's when I saw Jackie Chan movies. The thing that impressed so much is that Jackie could take anything and make it a prop. I would go home and practice that. I loved doing that. In *Irresistible Force* (1993), I'm in the kitchen using all the pots and pans to defend myself. I love that. To me, that's creativity. It's fun. Maybe someone would say, "That's not realistic," but if you hit someone in the head with a pan it's going to hurt.

Chris: Do props like that ever prove difficult to handle despite your weapons training?

Cynthia: I'm sure something was difficult along the way. I think the strong weapons background made it easier. If you give me something that's similar, like an umbrella is similar to a staff, you can adapt to it. Some of the moves were difficult, but not really the prop. That was just because the move was complicated.

Chris: Do you see yourself as a representative of feminism?

Cynthia: I'm totally for women going out there and doing it. I don't want to come across as thinking males are stronger. I wouldn't feel bad hurting a guy as much as a woman. Michelle Yeoh was really tough. I think women can do everything. I don't think women are the weaker of the sexes. The ones I had to fight have not been as used to taking contact. I think I am a representative though. When I started doing films, I was always the girlfriend. In the end of the movie, the guy would come in and save me. Why can't I be the hero and save myself? Well, women don't sell that well in the movie industry. It changed when I did *Sworn to Justice* (1996). I was the female hero, and I was glad not having to be saved by the guy. It's nice to show that you don't really need someone to do that. You do it yourself.

Chris: What do you believe makes up a Bad Ass Woman of Cinema?

Cynthia: An example of a bad ass woman in cinema is someone that can defend herself. Any woman you see in cinema is going to be bad ass because she is doing exactly that. Some people are stronger than others. Some look like that they couldn't do it, like if they get an actress without martial arts abilities. You'll look at it and think, "That wouldn't work." You have to make it look like it's effective, whether you can do it or not. Some women bad asses would be Angelina Jolie. I just saw *Salt* (2010). I was impressed with her athletic ability. There was a lot that she did. She was a bad ass in it. You could take someone like Michelle Yeoh or one of the other Hong Kong stars. They'd be bad ass because of the amazing movements.

Chris: Do you feel like having the representation of a strong woman is important?

Cynthia: Totally. Even with my daughter, I try to instill in her that you have to be strong both mentally and physically. I think that's a characteristic that everyone should achieve and strive for.

BETSY
RUSSELL

BEFORE BETSY RUSSELL TURNED EIGHTEEN, SHE WAS A WORKING actress. BETSY got enough work that she made the move to Los Angeles, and the risky move paid off. Betsy received small roles in television shows such as *The Powers of Matthew Star* (1982) that would pay the bills until her break came in the cult comedy *Private School* (1983). The film costarred Phoebe Cates and Matthew Modine but launched Russell's career. She would get high-level guest-starring roles on the hit shows *The A-Team*, *Family Ties*, and *T. J. Hooker*. More importantly, Betsy would get the lead role in two movies that continue to be cult favorites. First, she would star in the film *Tomboy* (1985). Betsy plays a self-reliant woman who has to win a race against her dream man to get any respect. Also

Betsy Russell in *Avenging Angel*.

in 1985 was the cult classic *Avenging Angel*. In this sequel, Betsy plays a former prostitute who is studying law. Unfortunately, the cop that helped her leave the street life is shot, and Angel takes up a gun for revenge. The two 1985 films show Betsy's range, and that she's able to carry a lead role. As Betsy's career was booming, she married Vincent Van Patten and decided to leave the business to raise her children. Years later, Betsy would return to the big screen in the *Saw* series. The horror franchise would introduce her to a new fanbase, garner interest in her past films, and resurrect her career.

Notable roles
Avenging Angel
Tomboy
The *Saw* series

Chris: How would you describe your childhood?
Betsy: I would describe my childhood as very unusual. I have an autistic sister who is five years older than I am. We had a lot of people who lived with us, taking care of my sister around the clock. It was sort of like a commune. My sister has never spoken a word in her life. It was unusual, and then my parents got divorced when I was about eleven. My mom bought this big property that had been a church. There was a church and a fellowship hall and dormitory; it was not a normal house. All I wanted to do was be normal, live in a normal house, and all that. I had a lot of love from a lot of people. My mother was always there with me, and my dad was really close by. All these surrogate people were helping to raise me. So, I did have a lot of love, and I could pursue whatever I wanted. I could try a new school or pursue acting. I could be in plays. My mom gave me so much freedom to be whoever I wanted to be and express myself. I was always writing poetry too. I really loved writing when I was a

little girl. I was writing a lot of poetry that I might turn into a book someday. It was different.

Chris: What type of child would you consider yourself to be?

Betsy: I was definitely the opposite of a tomboy. I was very prissy. I didn't want to get my hair messed up because I had this crazy, frizzy hair. God forbid I should go into the ocean, sweat, or do anything like that, because who knows what kind of hair day I was going to have. I was really worried about my appearance. I wore make up at an early age. I was very, very prissy. I wouldn't consider myself adorable or cute, but then when I got to be eleven or twelve people started commenting, "Oh, you've got such a cute nose or face." My body was starting to be very womanly. By the time I was thirteen/fourteen, I was coming into my own, getting noticed by boys. My mom says that when boys started noticing me is when I got happy. I was very outgoing. I wasn't the shy type. If some new kid came to the school I would always befriend her if she was cute and I got along with her.

Chris: Most actresses known for stronger female roles would not be described as a "prissy" child. How do you think the strong female roles came about despite your "prissy" childhood.

Betsy: *Tomboy* is the only role I would consider to be the opposite. I am a really strong personality. I've always been told I'm a leader, and I think I always have been. I don't think I'd be very convincing if I played the sweet, shy girl. I guess I could do it, but I haven't been offered those type of roles yet. Maybe when I'm older.

Chris: Were you athletic when you were younger?

Betsy: I did workout. When I turned around fifteen I noticed that these womanly curves were getting a little too curvy. I started working out, training, teaching aerobics. I became a workout fanatic. We were doing running in P.E. and I liked it. When I moved to Los Angeles, at seventeen, I became an avid runner. It got to the point that I was running nine miles a day. After I was married, I started playing tennis. Growing up, I would say I was athletic. I worked out before it was cool; I worked out with my stepmom. She had some funny machine where you get on all fours and do some weird type of exercise. I would exercise before school every day. I still work out at least five days a week. Exercise for me has been my drug. It helps when I'm feeling down or lack energy. That's been the most amazing gift.

Chris: What drew you to acting?

Betsy: I've never said this before, but I think it was almost an escape for me. I liked to pretend I was another person. I liked to pretend that I was Lucy, Cher, and Marlo Thomas. Looking back, in a new perspective, I felt (like I was) the only little girl in this sea of adults in my house; I really wanted to feel normal, and I loved all these shows with these women. Lucy was in a family. Marlo Thomas was married. It was all very normal and I wanted to pretend I was this normal girl in a normal family. It let me pretend I'm this person and that person, and I got to sample how that feels. It's not like my childhood was terrible, but it wasn't what I wanted it to be. I wanted to have normal sisters that weren't autistic, and I didn't want my friend's parents to say they couldn't come over because they were scared of my sister. It was all very unsettling for me. I liked the idea of being somebody else and the attention that came with it. I always liked people looking at me. I like to make people feel things. If I could make the audience feel something, as I did when I was watching a movie or television show, then that was great.

Chris: *Tomboy* had your character as a mechanic. How did this occupation change your character from a typical character?

Betsy: It defined her. I was playing a girl who loves auto mechanics. My oldest sister was a mechanic growing up. She did all the lube jobs on the car—she was that type of person. It wasn't far out for me to imagine myself as that type of character. That's what she did. She was a tomboy who liked riding motorcycles and playing basketball.

Chris: What are your thoughts on the trailer for *Tomboy* showing you as a strong female, but then cutting to you in the shower?

Betsy: I've never really paid attention to that. I don't know that I've seen it. I guess strong females still have to take showers. They still like to feel sexy, so I don't think there's one thing that should stop someone from feeling sexy and showing their body if that's what they choose to do. I don't think it makes any difference in the world.

Chris: *Tomboy* is arguably feminist. Was this a draw for you?

Betsy: Yes, I like playing strong characters. I thought it would be fun. I was probably twenty-one years old, so the idea of playing this type of character was great. I didn't think that hard about it. I said, "Ok, this is another role, this is what she does, and I'm going to get into it." I started working with the assistant basketball coach at UCLA, trying to learn a little bit of basketball. At that point in my life I wasn't thinking that long or hard about which role to take. I did have a couple of offers with *Tomboy*; I had another offer for another movie. I picked this one. I'm sure that was a draw for me.

Chris: What do you think makes it a feminist role?

Betsy: She has a career that isn't the norm for women. Usually women rely on men to do all the mechanical things. It's kind of unusual for a woman to be a mechanic. I think it's silly to be unusual, but I guess it is.

Chris: In the same vein, what role does feminism play in *Avenging Angel*?

Betsy: I barely remember that movie, but I know Angel carries a gun. She's a tough chick. I saw that movie maybe one time. I don't remember it well, but I had a lot of fun doing it.

Chris: They recently played it at a revival theater in Los Angeles.

Betsy: They did? I'll have to check it out. I don't know where they play these movies. My fans know way more than I would ever know. It's funny to me.

Chris: There were a couple of stronger roles you did early on. Did you find yourself drawn to the stronger roles?

Betsy: Typically the leads in movies are stronger women. Nobody wants to watch a wimp for two hours. I played more of a leading lady than the sidekick. I don't think I've ever played the sidekick. If given the chance, I would have. I did what I thought was good.

Chris: How did you get your role in *Avenging Angel*?

Betsy: I auditioned first, but then the director fought for me. The producer wanted the girl from the first movie. The director said he wouldn't do the movie without me. That was nice.

Chris: The *Saw* series?

Betsy: I was friends with the producers and started out as a three second role. I had really quit acting. Marc Berg, my fiancée at the time, asked me if I wanted to do a small part in this movie. I said, "Sure, why not? " It's one day's work, and I was going to be in Canada anyway with him. I did it. Then Marcus and Patrick, the writers, said they were going to put me as a big character in *Saw IV* if they got picked to write the movie. They got picked to write the movie. Jigsaw needed a female in his past life. They decided to write it that way. They were very kind to bring me back into acting. I'm grateful.

Chris: Did you ever turn down a role?

Betsy: I've turned down roles. If I thought the project was not written well or the character didn't have anything redeeming about her or I didn't feel it was right for me, I would turn it down. I've turned down roles in my twenties and, even, recently.

Chris: What would you say are your favorite type of roles?

Betsy: I really loved every character I've played. In *Chain Letter* (2009) I played a detective and now I'm about to play an FBI agent. I like playing strong, smart women. I'd really love to do comedy. I haven't shown any of that yet. I really want to show my comedic side. That would be a lot of fun. I did a play that was a comedy; it was the most fun I've ever had. It was Off Broadway. Maybe I'll do that again on stage someday.

Chris: Do you remember having a favorite line from *Avenging Angel*?

Betsy: No, but a lot of people tell me their favorite line from it, and I don't remember anything.

Chris: Tell me about filming the bareback riding scene in *Private School*.

Betsy: That was the scene where the director came to me a week into shooting, saying, "We are adding a scene if you're up for it." I said, "Oh, great, what is it?" He said, "You're going to be riding topless on this horse, enticing Phoebe Cates boyfriend Mathew Modine, trying to make her jealous." I said, "Excuse me? I'm going to be topless on a horse?" He said, "Yeah, but we think it's going to be a great scene." I said, "Well, I guess I'll do it if it's in slow motion and my helmet flies off. I want it to look like a beauty shot. If you do that, I guarantee it'll be memorable." It was. I remember everyone I didn't ever want to see again showing up on set that day.

Chris: What are your views on nudity in film?

Betsy: I don't have any negative views on it at all. In my twenties, I would say, "If it's intrinsic to the character then I think it's great." I learned that word, intrinsic, just to say that. I really don't have any problem with it. If it's just thrown in there because it's a low-budget movie and they're trying to sell it, it's really obvious. It takes you out, which isn't always great. Sometimes it's just right for what's going on. It's great that the actor or actress isn't embarrassed to show it. If it looks good then it's great. If it's a person who looks terrible I would rather they keep their clothes on. If it's important to the role and that type of film then it's fine.

Chris: What were your thoughts on *Cheerleader Camp* (1988) and *Camp Fear* (1991) and how have these thoughts evolved over time?

Betsy: *Camp Fear* was somebody called me and said, "Would you and your husband, Vince, like to do this little movie? You're going to make a lot of money for three weeks shoot, and it's going to go right to video." I said, "Great, I want to make a lot of money. If nobody sees it, I guess it doesn't matter. It'll be fun to work with my husband." We did it. Who knew that YouTube would happen. I've never seen the movie, so I have no idea. I'm sure I was terrible in it. It would be hard to be anything but terrible in it. I've always seen bits and pieces on YouTube. My voice is really high in it. We had fun. My brother-in-law is in that movie. I remember the actor playing the Indian could never remember his lines; we laughed so hard we almost fell off a cliff. That guy who played the Indian asked Vince to be his best man at his wedding. We barely knew him so that was funny. That happened back when they would say, "No one's ever going to see it." You'd do it. As an actor, if you're not working, you want to just work. It doesn't matter all of the time if it's best project if you haven't worked in a while. You have to put some money in the bank. That's why I did that. *Cheerleader Camp*, I hadn't worked in a while. At that time, not working in a while was a year or two. I got offered this role called *Bloody Pom Pom's* at the time. I remember thinking, "Oh my gosh, I don't have to take any clothes off." At that time, coming from *Private School, Tomboy*, and *Out of Control* (1985), I was tired of taking my clothes off. I wore those big nightgowns, and I just wanted to be taken seriously. That's why I did that movie. I had a lot of fun filming it. As for *Cheerleader* Camp, we didn't know we were making kind of a farce. Honestly, it was a little bit funny, but I took my character very seriously. We were rewriting scenes on the set five minutes before. It was a silly, little, low-budget movie. That's all it was. It wasn't supposed to be anything more than that. My sister called me before I did *Saw*, probably five years ago, and said, "They're playing *Cheerleader Camp* on the side of a building." I said, "Why?" She said, "I think it's this cult type of movie." I had no idea. I had basically quit acting and didn't think anyone cared about those movies. Even though I did a few movies with my ex-husband, I was taking care of my kids and not thinking about my acting career. So, for her to tell me they were playing this movie on the side of a building cracked me up. That's when I realized people really like that kind of movie. When I met Darren Lynn Bousman, he said, "You have to sign this for me." It was a DVD for *Cheerleader Camp*. I don't really know why people like it. Is it because it's so silly? It has a lot of the 1980s silly slasher elements. A lot of Playmates were in it too. They were all living in one house, and I got my own house. I said, "I don't want to be with them. I have to concentrate. I'm the lead of the movie." I thought I was doing *The Godfather* (1972) or something. I was really taking it seriously.

Chris: For a long time, *Camp Fear* was considered a lost film. Do you know the details of what happened?

Betsy: Meaning it's not anymore?

Chris: I watched it on Netflix Instant.

Betsy: Are you kidding me?

Chris: No.

Betsy: I have Netflix . I can watch it? That's hilarious. Is it awful?

Chris: It's not good.

Betsy: Why do they even have it there? I don't get it.

Chris: I was actually curious what your thoughts were on the cover. Across the top, in really big letters, is your name.

Betsy: I guess because I did *Saw*, they figure that's going to sell it and people are going to want to see the most terrible thing I ever did— that I always thought wouldn't come out. That's pretty funny. I've got to see it and laugh. The funniest part is that my kids have never seen anything I've ever done. At some point, they're probably going to watch everything and laugh.

Chris: What did the cast think when they were making it? Some things I noted while watching it: the earthquake, some sort of monster in the water that looked like a parade float, and then there was the Frankenstein-esque Indian.

Betsy: Vince and I were like, "This is the stupidest thing ever." We were trying to make our characters believable. We were just taking the money and running. Honestly, we didn't think it would ever be seen. You never really thought it would be seen by anybody. There wasn't YouTube or Netflix. I thought it was going in a can and never come out. So many movies did that before. If I hadn't done *Saw*, I don't think it ever would have come out. It would have stayed lost and maybe it should have. I don't regret anything I've done. I think it's funny, and I have to see it now. That's hilarious.

Chris: Was there any conversation about the rapist biker getting the girl at the end of the movie?

Betsy: The movie was really sort of a joke. I don't think there was a lot of thought put into any of it. I wasn't thinking, "Oh my God, I'm never going to work again." It wasn't porno or anything. What the heck? I barely read the script and haven't seen it, but that's definitely not cool.

Chris: I read some other interviews where you talked about the positive message that you saw in the *Saw* movies. I found that really interesting and wanted you to elaborate on that.

Betsy: I come from a spiritual and psychology background. I do believe that we're put on earth for a reason. It's our job to figure out our purpose and why we're here. A lot of times, people can't figure it out, so they walk around in a fog trying to say, "What the heck am I here for? What's my purpose?" Maybe Jigsaw had the idea that he was there to help people appreciate what they had. You know how things can be pretty terrible one day and you find the thing suddenly lifted? Whatever you were so worried about didn't actually happen and you feel so relieved after? You have to admit that these people he put in the horrible traps got a new perspective on life. In my mind, that's what Jigsaw was trying to do. Of course, it's not the right way to go about it. Then again, if the outcome is that you appreciate what you've got in every moment and you're not taking anything for granted, then that does wake us up. He had cancer, realized that he was going to die. When I was eighteen, I had a cancer scare. I had a lump on my foot and for a few weeks they didn't know if it was malignant or not. For those three weeks, my whole perspective on life changed a million percent. I never went back to my old way of thinking. Everybody I saw on TV, I would think, "They're so lucky because they get to live this full life." I would look at an old person and think, "How can they live this whole life and I may not?" As soon as I found out it wasn't malignant, I was so appreciative of every day of my life. I didn't pay attention to the little things that I didn't think were positive. Spiritual psychology is taking all the challenges that happen to us every day. You can look at those traps Jigsaw set as a challenge and turn it around, using it for our growth and learning experience. You can use it to look at things that happen to use every day. There's the things we think, "Oh, that's horrible that that happened." If you think, "Wait a minute. What am I supposed to be learning from this?" If you look at it that way then you're usually not going to be miserable. That was an interesting perspective for me because otherwise it was just evil and negative. I choose to see the positive in everything.

Chris: Do you think it takes a depiction of violence to make a point?

Betsy: No, I don't. I think people like to watch violence. It gets their adrenaline flowing, and they enjoy watching gore.

Chris: How has the making of each *Saw* film differed for you personally?

Betsy: The director changed. I felt more comfortable each film I did. A lot did stay the same. Every year is different. Every experience is different. I felt like my character grew each time. I approached my acting the same every time. There are always a few changes and the biggest was the director. The last one being in 3D was different. The procedure took so much longer to set up a shot.

Chris: What do you think about the direction your character went?

Betsy: I think they kept her integrity. She was really following Jigsaw's wishes. It would've been nice not to die. I would've loved to turn the whole thing around. I'm glad that, even though she tried to kill Hoffman, it wasn't because I became this horrible killer. In my mind, I was trying to end the whole thing. The fact that it didn't work and I ended up getting killed instead was a little typical, so I wish that hadn't happened. Everyone in a series wishes they hadn't died, though.

Chris: What are your thoughts on being in several cult classics, and did you think they would still be watched today?

Betsy: I never thought about the longevity of the movies. The cool thing about being an actor is that you realize, "This is going to be here forever." My kids could see it, my grandkids. It's like you never die. For me, it's pretty awesome to think I'm leaving a piece of me on earth. At the same time, I never really thought about whether people would still be watching it. I did the best I could and moved on. I got into acting thinking I would be doing this until I die. When I did give it up to raise my kids and it seemed over, I thought, "Wow, this isn't how I thought it would go." I tried to get back into it when my kids got older, but you don't realize when you quit that it's such a difficult business. Taking time off and then trying to come back, competing against all the people who never had kids or took time off. They are going to get the jobs before you do. I was lucky to make a comeback. I'm just hoping people will enjoy my work for a long time.

Chris: Who do you consider to be a Bad Ass Woman of Cinema and why?

Betsy: Angelina Jolie would be the first one to mind. She plays those type of roles, and I think she's a fabulous actress. She's very physical. I think she's number one in my book.

CATHERINE MARY
STEWART

CATHERINE MARY STEWART HAS A VARIED CAREER. AT THE AGE OF seven she began studying dance. Later, Catherine would go on an international tour with the Synergy Dance Company. Catherine would graduate high school and then move to London to study both dance and theater. Attending an audition with some friends would offer Catherine her first big break in the film *The Apple* (1980). She would take a chance and try out Hollywood. In the early 1980s, Catherine took the role of Kayla Brady on the long-running soap opera *Days of Our Lives*. With her acting career started, Catherine seemed to get varied roles in movies that would live on in midnight shows. The year of 1984 brought the Nick Castle cult classic *The Last Starfighter* (1984). That same year brought

Regina (Catherine Mary Stewart) patrols the streets in *Night of the Comet*. Photo courtesy of Atlantic Releasing Corporation

Stewart and Kelli Maroney as sisters having fun in an empty world, until they have to fend off zombies in *Night of the Comet* (1984). Catherine would go on to star in numerous TV-movies, guest star on TV shows like *The Outer Limits*, and appear in comedies such as *Dudes* (1987) and *Weekend at Bernie's* (1989). More recently, Catherine returned to the stage for *A Christmas Snow* (2010) and regularly attends conventions.

Notable roles
Night of the Comet
The Last Starfighter
The Apple
Dudes

Chris: How did you go from studying dance to film?

Catherine: I was attending a performing arts school in London, England. On my way to class one morning, I bumped into a couple of classmates who were on their way to an audition they had heard about. I decided to tag along, totally unprepared for what I was about to experience. It was a cattle call audition for the *The Apple*. During the dance portion of the audition, I noticed the director framing me with his fingers while he watched. Long story short, he took me out of the group. He had me sing and read for him. Within the week I was cast as the lead in a feature film.

Chris: Were you naturally comfortable in front of the camera?

Catherine: I guess so. I don't really remember thinking too much about it. Everything happened pretty quickly. I suppose I was a bit distracted with keeping up with the whirlwind that I was living.

Chris: You were on the soap opera *Days of Our Lives* for a couple of years. Many actors have a difficult time transitioning. What do you feel was different for you?

Catherine: I think in many ways I was fortunate not to have been on the show too long. There is a definite technique to soap acting that doesn't necessarily translate. On the other hand, there have been incredibly successful actors who got their start in soaps. I admire soap actors. It was the hardest job I've ever had.

Chris: In *Scenes from the Goldmine* **(1987), it shows the inner happenings of a band on the rise. Have you seen this type of behavior or these happenings in the film business?**

Catherine: Yes! I always had a great experience in my career, but I think I consciously chose a path that kept me relatively sane in this sometimes crazy business. I was happy to keep my work life and my personal or social life separate. The people who surrounded me were honest, protective, and professional. I never felt like I compromised myself or had to compromise myself. But, like I said, it was a conscious decision.

Chris: What type of person would you say it takes to make it in the film business?

Catherine: Determined, professional, educated in the business on every level possible, and prepared.

Chris: You starred in several films that required musical talent. How much musical background did you have?

Catherine: I've always been very musical. Of course, as a dancer it's an essential element. I was also involved in musical theatre through my early years. I love music of every kind, and I love to sing! It's a passion of mine.

Chris: How much training did those type of roles require for you?

Catherine: Training your singing voice is similar to training as an actor. They are instruments that need to be practiced and used to stay flexible. I've studied both over the years. I'm preparing now for a new musical stage performance of a movie I did recently called *A Christmas Snow* in Branson, Missouri. I'm excited.

Chris: Tell me about working with Rutger Hauer in *Nighthawks* **(1981).**

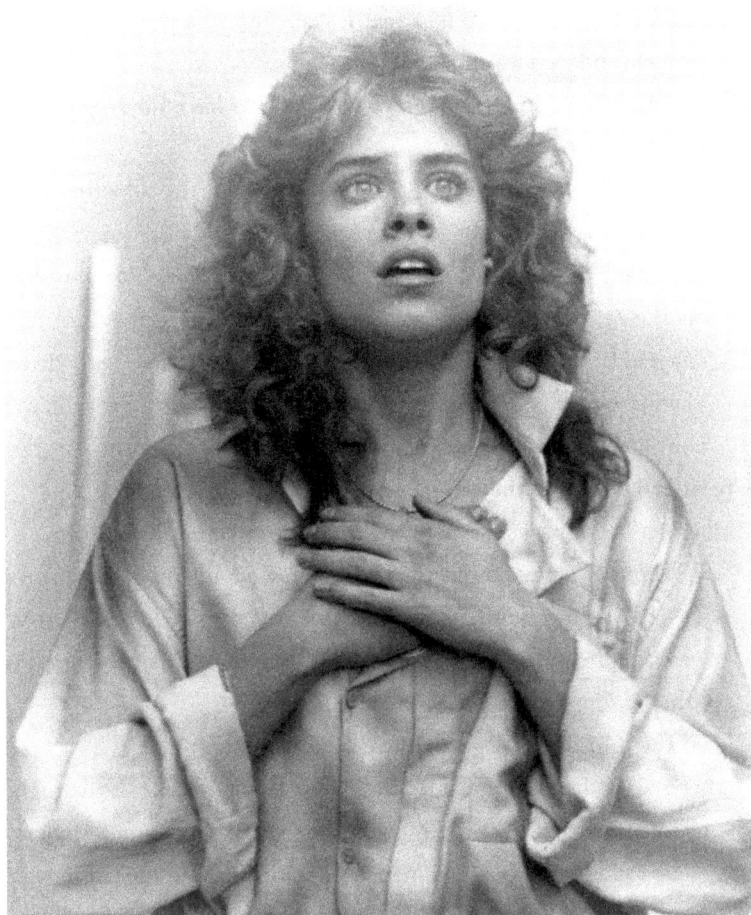

Reggie (Catherine Mary Stewart) is startled by the changes
in the world after the dramatic *Night of the Comet*.
Photo courtesy of Atlantic Releasing Corporation

Catherine: He was scary! I think he was staying in character on and off
camera. He didn't speak to me much, but he totally intimidated me.

**Chris: What are your thoughts of *Night of the Comet* being viewed as
symbolizing female independence?**

Catherine: I think it's cool. I love that it portrayed two young women
who, although they had the sensibilities of young teenage girls, were
still capable of looking after themselves. You don't see that very often

in film. I've heard from fans that it really influenced them as young women, and guys totally dig it too.

Chris: What weapons training did you need to have for *Night of the Comet*?

Catherine: We were taken to a firing range to practice shooting Mac 10s. We learned all about them and how they work. It's really so important to know and understand weapons that you are shooting on the set. Even though you are shooting blanks, they are very dangerous and you need to be completely responsible with them. There are fifty people on the set who are put in harm's way if you don't know what you're doing or you don't take it seriously.

Chris: Tell me about the Uzi scene in *Night of the Comet*.

Catherine: The guns were actually Mac 10s. They jammed fairly often so the director/writer, Thom Eberhardt threw in a line for Sam where she says in frustration, "Dad would have got us Uzis." It was when we were shooting at a car and the gun kept jamming. My response was "The car didn't know the difference..."

Chris: The "Girls Just Want to Have Fun" scene.

Catherine: We had a lot of fun. We shot it in the middle of the night in some big mall in Los Angeles. First of all, talk about a fantasy scene for a lot of young women. When it turns into the battle with the zombies it was kind of cool. Squibs blasting off everywhere! Fun stuff!

Chris: What attracted you to the role?

Catherine: I think the strength of the character of Reggie. I was labeled, at that time, as the "girl next door" actress. This was a departure from that characterization and much more like the real me. It was also unusual to read a script where two female characters are the lead and, as I mentioned earlier, can actually look after themselves. What I think also makes it work is the fact that there was a real vulnerability to these young women, but that didn't paralyze them as is so often portrayed with female characters.

Chris: What message do you think *The Last Starfighter* carries?

Catherine: Follow your dreams, even if involves a battle! It's worth it in the end. Go for what scares you and challenges you. It's so satisfying to conquer your fears.

Chris: How did you view getting so many roles in genre films when many actors shy away from doing them?

Catherine: I guess in retrospect I did a number of sci-fi movies, but I think it was also a sign of the times. Mostly, I looked at the story and the character. If it moved me on some level I would pursue it. I suppose some actors don't want to be pigeon holed, but I wasn't concerned with that. I love to work.

Chris: What preparation did you do for your role in *Dudes*?

Catherine: Oh, I loved doing that movie. I love riding and shooting. I loved westerns growing up and fantasized about riding full out across the plains or the desert. We did some riding and a lot of gunplay to prepare. I learned to twirl that gun and have it land in my holster and do that quick shooting at the bottles. One of my favorite scenes was when I took off on the horse and galloped across a field towards the camera. It was an absolutely beautiful setting. Unfortunately, someone had parked their jeep right behind the camera that I was galloping towards. The horse wouldn't turn until the last second, and I went flying off into the jeep. I broke my arm! That was wild but kind of cool. Fortunately, it was towards the end of the shoot, so I was put in a cast that could be removed for the subsequent shots. I also had some good pain killers.

Chris: "I'm not a whore, George. Don't treat me like one," is a line from *World Gone Wild* (1988). What did this mean for your character?

Catherine: The challenging thing to me about *World Gone Wild* was: How do I, as an actress, express the innocence, vulnerability, curiosity, yet authority of someone who is starting with a clean slate and trying to create a civilized society within this small group? This was a community of people who were not only trying to survive in these dire circumstances but also my character, as a "teacher," was trying to bring some civility to the children particularly, and to live in a culture that she knew nothing about. Somehow, given the chaos of the world, the foundation of this has been erased, and anyone who may have had knowledge of it was either totally wacko at this point or dead. She had a perception of how previous generations lived, long ago, based on movies that she'd watched or novels that she had read. So how do I express that through my character? Everything the character said was as though she was reading from a studied script without any background as to why she would say it. The "I'm not a whore" line was probably a line from some movie that the character had seen and that had reflected the uncomfortable circumstance that she found herself in that moment.

Chris: What are your thoughts on *World Gone Wild*?

Catherine: I love themes that express survival on an almost animalistic level—survival of the fittest. I think it's the true nature of human beings. After all, we are animals. What separates us is that we possess that undeniable need to love and be loved. We are basically benevolent creatures. That's what makes us strong, ultimately. This was another film that I just loved shooting. The physical location was paradise for me.

Chris: In *Love N' Dancing* (2009) you play the aunt. How do you feel about getting the adult roles now? What are the positive/negative aspects of this?

Catherine: I find playing the older roles quite liberating. I've always looked much younger than I am, yet I always wanted to be older. Go figure. I've had a blast playing characters with more dimension and complexity in a way. Life gives you dimension, and it's really fun to express that.

Chris: Several of your films have become cult classics and have a life even today. Is there one film that you think deserves to be seen more than it has?

Catherine: One of my favorite projects was a mini-series I did with Armand Assante, Rod Steiger, Mariette Hartley, and a truly stellar cast, called *Passion and Paradise* (1989). I hate the title, but it was a really interesting story of politics, wealth, passion, and murder based on real events that happened at the dawn of the WWII. I wish it had more exposure. I was very proud of that piece.

Chris: Which character have you played who best represents who you are?

Catherine: They all have a bit of me in them. I'm pretty independent, opinionated, athletic, sassy, tough, sensitive, shy, and self-critical. I love the challenges of life. I feel so lucky to have had the life that I've had, and I have so much more that I want to do.

Chris: What do you believe makes a strong female character?

Catherine: Intelligence, thoughtfulness, independence, dimension, vulnerability.

Chris: What are your thoughts on being considered a sex symbol?

Catherine: I think it's cool! I certainly don't think of myself as a traditional sex symbol, but I suppose that can be sexy.

Chris: Have you ever felt the need to maintain this status?

Catherine: I've never thought of myself as having that "status," so I've never thought about maintaining it. I think a part of the roles I play involves maintaining a certain physical appearance. Or, perhaps, I demand that of myself. Those demands on myself inspire me to keep in shape, which is a win-win thing in terms of appearance and even more importantly, health.

Patricia Tallman in *Night of the Living Dead*

PATRICIA
TALLMAN

PATRICIA BEGAN ACTING WHEN SHE WAS A CHILD, APPEARING ON radio shows and performing live theatre, which would train her for the varied career to come. Patricia went from summer stock to earning a B.F.A. at Carnegie Mellon University, performing on the side at Pittsburgh Civic Light Opera. Patricia moved to New York City and began her professional career on Broadway before turning to television and movies. Legendary filmmaker George Romero would cast Patricia in *Knightriders* (1981). The pair would team up for several projects over the years, including the Romero produced remake of *Night of the Living Dead* (1990). The film is memorable for Patricia's wonderful portrayal of the heroic, bad ass Barbara. Her character starts off weak and helpless but arches into a shotgun-wielding loner, becoming, intentional or not, a cult feminist figure. Patricia would follow up *Night of the Living Dead* with supporting roles in *Dead Air* (2009) and the Hugo Award-winning *Babylon 5*. To sustain a career, Patricia did what several other interviewees did: she became a stuntwoman. Patricia performed stunts on numerous productions, including *Army of Darkness* (1992), *NCIS*, and *Austin Powers: International Man of Mystery* (1997).

Notable roles
Night of the Living Dead
Babylon 5
Knightriders

Chris: Describe your childhood.
Patricia: I grew up in rural Illinois. It was Central Illinois, kind of in the middle of nowhere. I had two younger sisters and a baby brother. We moved to the suburbs of Chicago, so I was a Midwestern girl.

Chris: Were you athletic?
Patricia: I've always been athletic. I like dancing and horseback riding. I didn't do any team sports. I wasn't into that.

Chris: How would you describe yourself as a child?
Patricia: I was very normal. I was like how all kids are. We're a little bit of everything, aren't we? We're curious and shy and outgoing all at the same time, depending on who you're with. I was pretty responsible. I was the oldest. I always loved animals and my family. I was pretty obsessed with horses. I really liked *Star Trek* (1966) and *Dark Shadows* (1966)—those were my two favorite shows. My cousin and I used to play with our Barbie dolls to *Star Trek* and *Dark Shadows*. I think that's indicative of somebody who's obsessed with science fiction and horror. It's not surprising that I ended up in those genres.

Chris: In high school you had starred in some musicals.

Patricia: High school is when I really started to do plays and things like that. *Bye, Bye Birdie* was the first musical I had a big part in. We did a lot of plays and then it was really until I was at college, working summers, that I got into it. I was in residence at Pittsburgh Civic Light Opera. I did eleven musicals in ten weeks—it was crazy. That's when I really started doing musicals.

Chris: Would you consider it an interest for you to do musicals?

Patricia: I didn't consciously set out to be in musicals. Doing a musical, especially when starting out in high school, is a normal part of theater repertoire. If you notice, every theater company will have a musical. Usually it's in the summer. I don't know why. Everybody always works it in some capacity in every show. So I just ended up doing musicals. It's not that I'm a great singer or dancer or anything. I enjoyed it, though.

Chris: Did that training help you at all in the future?

Patricia: I think doing any show is going to help you. You develop your skills, understanding of theater, stagecraft, and just get better at what you do. Musicals made me more interested in dancing and rhythm. When I branched off into doing stunts I understood rhythms and fights and was very good with my body because I had been a dancer.

Chris: How did you get involved with *Knightriders*?

Patricia: I was in New York City and I heard about the audition through friends. I somehow got the audition. I may have got help from my agent. I don't remember how I got the audition. I auditioned for George Romero in New York City. I got the part. I ended up going back to Pittsburgh. I went to college in Pittsburgh. I moved to New York, and that year I got the job and had to go back to Pittsburgh. I shot there for the summer.

Chris: Your character is a small town girl who ends up taking off with the *Knightriders*. As you leave, your mother has been beaten up. How do you view your character in *Knightriders*?

Patricia: I was a teenager in *Knightriders*. I got out of a bad situation. My mother didn't stand up for me or for herself. Now, I'm not sure if you mean should I stay home and confront my father and try to save my mother, but I think that anyone who gets out is doing the right thing. You can't look back and say, "God, I should have…" I don't know how you can, especially a child. Parents saving their children are expected. It was good that she got out.

Chris: Were you apprehensive about doing the topless scene?

Patricia: Yes. I didn't want to do it. Now I don't care at all. I don't think nudity should be a big deal. I think bodies are bodies. It's so funny, but I think I was more nervous about what my parents would think. Having done so much theater, where everyone's whipping their clothes on and off backstage trying to get in and out of costumes, it was no big deal. Half the time you're working with people who are gay and not interested in you anyway. I wasn't terribly modest, but I didn't want to be judged, so it was a new world for me. Nobody was taking me under their wings and saying, "This is how we do nudity." I was just thrust into the situation, and it was my first time in front of a camera. I really had no idea or how to handle myself. Once I saw it I was OK with it.

Chris: What did you learn from George Romero?

Patricia: I learned it was OK to have opinions and make choices. I learned how to respectfully talk to the director and that I was welcome to. He made me very welcome to give ideas. Even though I was this kid, I was twenty-one, and he was a veteran, acclaimed filmmaker, he treated me like a colleague. I didn't know how marvelous it was. I just felt accepted, and it allowed me to really blossom on the set as an actress. It gave me confidence to give my best work at that time. He enabled me to do that, and I've learned since then how special he was.

Chris: Were you apprehensive about taking over the iconic Barbara role in *Night of the Living Dead*?

Patricia: No. Not at all. Not for a second. At first, I was confused as to why to remake the movie to begin with. At that time there weren't a lot of remakes. It was explained to me that George had a copyright issue. When he released what we think of as *Night of the Living Dead* (1968), it was released under the title *Night of the Flesheaters*. When the distribution company changed the name, they didn't copyright it. George was ripped off. People were releasing rip-offs of his movie, and he didn't ever make any money off of it. They came up with this idea that one way to stop that would be to copyright it, releasing a new movie under the very same name. Then George explained what the differences were going to be in this movie. There were the advances that had been made in special effects, we had Tom Savini, and Barbara was going to be a modern woman. We had only really seen that with Sigourney Weaver—she was the first one. I never looked back at all. I was very different from Judith O'Dea, a wonderful woman and great actress. Our characters were so different.

Chris: What did you try to bring to the role?

Patricia: Honesty. Barbara was a very ordinary woman. She got caught in an extraordinary circumstance. She fell apart for a while, and then found a way to deal with it. We can argue that she was strong or fell apart at the end. I just tried to be really honest.

Chris: Right off the bat at the cemetery, you are kicking zombie ass. Although you struggle with emotions at times, she comes off as a very strong character. What sort of direction did Savini give you for the role?

Patricia: Tom's a great director. He's very much an actor's director. He appreciates the process actors go through. He's respectful and gets excited. He's great to work with. I don't remember exactly our conversations, but I always felt that whatever I did he really liked, approved, and encouraged me. I did kick zombie ass in the graveyard. I was frantic and trying to get away. I was running and screaming so she just kept moving more than being strong. That's what I mean by being honest. I think that if that character resonated with people who came to see that movie it's because I tried to be truthful, and they believed that this ordinary person scraped her way through these moments to survive. They watched her evolve. It's very clear the moments where Barbara transitions. She just goes, "Okay, I'm not going to do this anymore." In the first scene with Tony Todd, in the farmhouse, she couldn't talk or articulate. To come back from that in a meaningful and real way that wouldn't be goofy or contrived, I'm very grateful that Tom helped me shape the performance. When you're an actor, you can't see what you're doing. You don't know if you're getting lost. You need to have a director that can help you craft a performance over two hours to make sense of the story.

Chris: Did you study the original movie at all?

Patricia: Nope. I don't like horror movies. I don't like zombies. I think they're messy and stinky. I like vampires; vampires are sexy. I'm not a big fan of gore. I like scary movies like *The Haunting* (1963). I like ghost stories but not monsters. It freaks me out. I had bad nightmares almost every day on that shoot. It was during the day. We were like vampires by working all night and sleeping all day. I had bad dreams every day.

Chris: The original *Night of the Living Dead* is arguably viewed as a statement on racism. The version you starred in would be closer to a feminist statement. How do you view that?

Patricia: I didn't think of the political ramifications at all. That's because I had a role to consider. That job is for the producers and director. They wanted to create an idea, especially with the type of character I was. I thought it was much more important to be honest because the script was well done. I didn't need to put in anything that wasn't there. Yes, in the end, I think you're right. It did have much more of a feminist point of view. Barbara turns out to be a hero if only because she survives. She overcomes. In that sense, she's kind of a hero.

Patricia Tallman with fan at a convention.
Photo courtesy of Brian Wilson.

I didn't set out to make her a hero or have any of that self-awareness about her at all. I don't think that would have worked.

Chris: Even in the relationship between Tom Towles and his wife, Tom wants to hide and the wife wants to come help you.

Patricia: Yeah, exactly. That's what I mean about it being well-written. She wasn't real successful. There were some nice things in there. It was just starting to become OK for women to start kicking butt a little bit. Sigourney Weaver in *Aliens* made that happen for us. It was something I always dreamed about, but I wanted to be Sigourney Weaver. I wanted to be in *Aliens*, not zombie movies. Zombies are gross.

Chris: What are your thoughts on the ending of *Night of the Living Dead*?

Patricia: I like that it's complicated. I like that it's not the way you thought it was going to go. I like that it's flawed, that she's disturbed and troubled. You've got to be a little disturbed and troubled to be shooting someone in the head, even if they are a creepy guy. I always like it when characters are not black-and-white. That's one of the things I loved about *Babylon 5*. Just when you knew where a character was, they went to the other side. That made it really fun.

Chris: In *Army of Darkness*, you play a possessed witch. What challenges did playing this role present?

Patricia: Surviving the makeup. That was my challenge. The guys at KNB Effects are amazing and wonderful. It was a four-hour makeup job. They cast my head. They had to create the hump, face and hands. I couldn't do anything for seventeen hours. No bathroom or eating. Then they put in these contact lenses. They were huge. They weren't made to fit my eyes. They were a general, milky contact lens. People would be holding me down to put the contact lenses back in my eyes. It was awful. When Bruce finally shoots me at the end, I was so happy to fall over. Sam says, "Do something at the end!" I take like seventeen squib hits. Bruce just swings that thing over his shoulder and starts shooting me. I was so exhausted and couldn't see anything with those lenses. I just fell over. I loved it. I got another lovely director. Bruce and Sam are amazing. They called me from their car phone after editing and they said, "You're our favorite monster!" I cherish that. It was really fun. It was fun making Sam excited. That was a rough shoot, though.

Chris: How does Sam Raimi differ from other directors you've worked with?

Patricia: They're all different. I think Sam was in a mode. You have to understand it's not like we're having tea. Everyone's working their butts off. I'm in one area being prepared in makeup. I have to be careful. I can't bump up against things. Sam and I come together to talk about what we need to do, and then we go back to dealing with other things. It's not like we're having meaningful conversations about life. We're just about the work. I'm working with the stunt coordinator and dealing with a rig. Sam would have to be close enough and loud enough to me because of all the makeup. He would try to express what his vision is. The witch is a case where I really was crafted by Sam. Of course I have ideas, but it's not like Barbara where I have an emotional life. With the witch I'm a character he's crafting. I'm fitting into his film. The action I need to give him, which is typical for a stunt person, you're typically trying to fulfill the vision of the filmmaker. The more you can bring their storyboard to life the more they love you. Being an actor as well I'm kind of a director's dream because I can give you the body language and the emotional life. I think that's part of what Bruce and Sam were responding to when they called me. With Sam, it was much more of a shot by shot collaboration. With Tom Savini, he would follow me around and see what I was doing, making suggestions on how to help the cinematography. We'd work on it that way and then bring the other actors in. There was a conversation together. Then he would create the camera moves and lighting and then we would break it all apart and shoot it. With Sam, it was "Okay, we're going to shoot this now." It may be out of order. It's the same scene, but we shoot what makes sense for Sam. It makes his job easier.

Chris: What are your thoughts on being involved in so many cult classics?

Patricia: Isn't it weird? I can only go back to what we talked about before. Being a little girl and visualizing *Dark Shadows* and then what do I end up in? How bizarre is that? I must have put something in motion at that time. I think we're also talking about genres that lend to themselves to becoming cult hits. Sure, you've got your *Easy Rider* (1969) and other kinds of films that become cult hits. Typically, I think science fiction and horror movies have more cult hits.

Chris: How do you view yourself as an actress? What do you think your strengths are? What do you use, if anything, to get yourself to where the character needs to be?

Patricia: I had some pretty remarkable people say that I was one of the most honest actors they knew. That means so much to me. I consider that an enormous compliment. I try to be very truthful. I don't know. Maybe I'm not that self-aware and should be. I can do anything. I wish I worked more.

Chris: How did you get into stuntwork?

Patricia: I fell into it (laughs). I took stage combat classes. I really loved it, and I was really good at it. I really enjoyed telling stories through action. I'm a great admirer of the old swashbucklers. I love Errol Flynn and Basil Rathbone. I still love action movies. I really love watching Jackie Chan. There's something to being able to do that. I was taking pyramid sword technique classes in New York City— it's such a geeky thing to do. I met some stunt people in that class. I was in class a couple of months, and we were at broadswords at that point. One of the guys was a stunt coordinator and he said, "I need someone who's five-feet-nine to fall down the stairs. Would you do that?" I was like, "Yeah." So, I was playing an actress in lingerie, which means there's no place to put any pads. I had to fall down some stairs and hit marks. It turned out I was really good at it. I made some really good money that day. I thought it was amazing. Because I was a good size and type, I could double a lot of actresses. I just started building a career. I didn't set out to be a stunt person at all. It turned out to be something I was really good at. I made good money in my union; it's still Screen Actors Guild. I was on sets and learning my craft. I was able to hang out with other actors. It's great.

Chris: That might answer my follow up question. Why continue in stunt work when you've had significant roles in feature films and television?

Patricia: We make money. I need to make money, everyone does. It's funny that there's perspective people think actors have so much money, which we don't. We get paid a normal salary if we're working. If we're not working, we're not making money. Residuals are pretty much dried up for my industry, so that doesn't happen anymore. If I get an offer for a job, I'll do it. I did one on *Castle* last fall. That was really fun. I found Nathan Fillion was a fan of mine. That was the highlight of my year.

Chris: What do you consider to be your most notable stuntwork?

Patricia: In *Long Kiss Goodnight* (1996), I did some pretty harrowing things. They were definitely life-threatening. I had my baby by then. I had him with me when I was in Toronto shooting. When I was hanging upside down, eighty feet over the camera in a rock quarry outside Toronto in the middle of a freezing cold night, the cable was going to drop me in front of the camera freefall. I was thinking if this cable goes wrong I'm dead and my little boy is being taken care of by a nanny. What am I doing? It was one thing when I was single but another thing when you've got a kid. I really dialed it back after that.

Chris: What injuries have you sustained from doing stuntwork?

Patricia: I've had multiple concussions. I broke my back twice. I've got scars. The worst part right now that I'm living with is some chronic pain and arthritis. It's like being a football player; you take impact so many times that your joints can't handle it anymore. Your body responds in certain ways. I don't regret it all. I couldn't have created the life I have if I didn't do it, but you definitely pay a heavy toll for it. I don't think a lot of young people realize that. They just think of the glory of being a stuntman. Did you see *Karate Kid* (2010)? Did you see how Jackie Chan walks? He wasn't putting that on. It only gets worse.

Chris: What do you feel led to you being cast in stronger female roles?

Patricia: I am a stronger female. Essentially, as actors, except in the case of really nice people who play something like serial killers, I think that who we are is how we are cast. I think I am one. I think there's a lot of us. I'm also big at five-feet-nine. I'm not thin. I'm a big woman at size ten. That's big in this town. I'm physically imposing. I think that helps. I'm pretty direct. I have no interest in bullshit. I have no patience. I tend to be abrupt.

Chris: Do you feel satisfied with your career?

Patricia: No, I'm hungry. I want more. I don't know too many actors who are totally satisfied. Even if they're working all the time, they're going, "This role is the one I always wanted." I don't work all the time and that's a frustration for me. It makes me more creative, coming up with new things to do.

Chris: What do you believe makes a strong, female character?

Patricia: I'll go back to honesty again. Being honest, following through with your convictions and standing up for what you believe is really right. That's what makes them really strong.

Chris: Who do you consider to be a Bad Ass Woman of Cinema?

Patricia: I think we need more role models of bad ass women in their fifties and sixties. I don't think we have enough. Sigourney Weaver is still kicking ass, but we don't have enough. I'm going with the words "bad ass" so I think Helen Mirren has played characters where she's definitely kicking some ass. Then, there's Sigourney Weaver. There's actresses out there, working and surviving in this industry who are well into their fifties and sixties who aren't action or genre heroes, but they're still working to where I'd consider them formidable. It's not easy being a woman of, say, forty. It's not easy in this town. Everybody is botoxed and enhanced. I've resisted that so far and it's hard. It's hard watching yourself age and being ignored and marginalized. It happens every day. It's tough. I was just in the UK and treated very differently. Claudia Christian works in the UK for this very reason. She works more there. She's in her forties, but feeling the pain of being a woman in Hollywood. Just look at the BBC. You've got older characters with women who are the stars of the show. They aren't just the parents. They are the stars. We don't do that here—it's too bad.

CHRIS
YEN

CHRIS YEN LOOKS SMALL AND SWEET, BUT SHE'S REALLY A BUNDLE OF badassery. Spawned from the genes of legendary martial artist Bow Sim Mark and brother to Hong Kong superstar Donnie Yen, Chris is trying to make a name for herself. She grew up in Boston, training at her mother's kung fu school called "The Chinese Wushu Research Institute." Chris would compete in martial arts tournaments, winning numerous awards and accolades, but she also had the desire to pursue acting.

Chris Yen is not your standard actress. Casting directors have taken notice, casting Chris as both hero and villain. Sure, she's battled the bad guys in *The Adventures of Johnny Tao* (2007), but her more notable roles have come as the villain. In *The Black Rose* (2004) and *Give 'em Hell*

181

Photo courtesy of Chris Yen.

Malone (2009), Chris portrays venomous villains. As she did with martial arts, Chris began studying acting at a young age. She enrolled in a youth theater program at Emerson College. Still very young, Chris also got a role in the Yuen Woo Ping film *Close Encounter of a Vampire* (1986). Even at a young age and in a supporting role, Chris proved to have martial arts talent that translated to screen.

Chris Yen would prove to have more going on than just beauty and talent—she graduated from Boston College with degrees in both business and psychology. Despite her other career options, Hong Kong came calling again for the film *The Black Rose*, codirected by her brother Donnie Yen. Chris would get to show off her martial arts skills again as the highlight of *The Adventures of Johnny Tao*. However, Chris continues to branch outside of martial arts films with the Sundance selection *A Good Day to be Black and Sexy* (2008), *Give 'em Hell Malone*, and *Rockville CA* (2009). On top of acting, Chris has a slate of projects she's producing. Chris has a bright future both in front of and behind the camera.

Notable roles
The Black Rose
Give 'em Hell Malone
The Adventures of Johnny Tao

Chris Watson: How would you say growing up at your mom's kung fu school made your childhood different?

Chris Yen: At the time my mom had her martial arts school there was really nobody else around who was doing what she was doing, especially as a woman. My parents were new immigrants. We actually lived in a Jewish neighborhood while the school was situated in Chinatown. My life was split up between growing up in the Jewish community, being the only Asian girl in my school, and then growing up in Chinatown, being the only kung fu girl. On a personal level, that was definitely very different and challenging growing up during those times. That set me apart. I found the challenge came when I looked like everyone else. I felt like I could be like everyone else, but I was definitely seen differently because people saw me as the kung fu girl. When going around kids, I was always being challenged, especially by guys. People think, "Oh, kung fu? She must know how to fight. We need to challenge her." I was challenged a lot, both in school and the community surrounding my mom's dojo. I also had experiences with other students. That was very interesting because the majority of her students were Caucasian and black Americans. We had very few Asian students then. They came from all walks of life; there were professors, musicians, and even other martial arts types that came to study. They wanted to study internal arts from my mother. I was the youngest. Everyone around me was older so I grew up with a bunch of kung fu brothers; the majority of the students were men at the time. Overall, my childhood was different and colorful. It was fun because it was different. I was always surrounded by people of all sorts, ages, and backgrounds. At the same time, training was a daily routine for us. Like going to school, doing homework, and eating, it was normal for me. I didn't know that it wasn't normal for other people. I grew up trying to overcome some of those prejudices. It was something I had to deal with.

Chris Watson: What did your training consist of?

Chris Yen: We traditionally trained in Chinese martial arts, mainly Wushu and some of the internal arts. That's what my mother specialized in. The Wushu is a very broad form of martial arts that encompasses the touching and internal aspect, as well as the Shaolin aspect—the vigorous, physical aspect that consists of forms and various, long and short form weapons. That was the spectrum of our complete training. On a daily level it was Wushu, which incorporates very strong fundamentals of basic kicking, punching, and movements. Every day we would do the same routine. There's a set of kicks. There's a stretching routine. There's a set of punches. There's a set of sword routine we'd have to practice. Then we'd switch to a long staff routine. Then we'd switch to a broad sword routine. Daily, my training would incorporate the basics, then forms, and then weapons. It was a three to four hour minimum training every day after school. That was my experience at my mother's dojo, but I was also sent to China a couple of times when I was younger. That was a completely different kind of training schedule. That was an experience in of itself. I remember my first summer being sent there, I lived with the students that were a bunch of kids. We trained together six days a week, seven hours a day. It was like we were training for the Olympics or something. I remember feeling that way at the time. Someday maybe we're going to get Wushu into the Olympics. Maybe someday this is going be a much, much bigger event. At the time Wushu was relatively unknown. It certainly wasn't like it's popularized now.

Chris Watson: Was the purpose of being sent to China to get additional training?

Chris Yen: It was to get additional training on a different level because when I was training in my mom's school, I was the only kid. We didn't have that many kids around. I was also very fascinated because we used to get the videotapes sent to us of the Chinese Wushu team. I'd get to see some of the other girls and boys that were my age, doing the things that I'm doing. I'm seeing them do it at their level. They're trained completely different. My mom wanted me to have that experience under my belt to see what it was like to train alongside children my age. It would give me the experience of going back to my native country, to practice this national sport. I would have a completely different type of Wushu training.

Chris Watson: Do you believe this training helped you grow faster internally as a woman?

Chris Yen: That's a very complex question. Yes, definitely so. Internally, psychologically, spiritually, as a person, as a human being… it's given me the type of internal strength in discipline. That kind of training is something completely different. As a woman, especially growing up as a woman when I was younger, I never really understood the purpose of all this training. It was part of our lives. I never really questioned it because my family was doing it. When I was younger, I took a lot of this for granted. I had something so special and so unique. Growing up into adulthood, becoming a woman, wow... I often look back, look at my family, look at their successes, look at where I came from, and I have so much thanks to give, especially to my mother. I'm incredibly lucky to have been put into this position in this family. To have these skill sets and this gift has helped empower me. It has certainly helped to enrich me. Trying to use those experiences that I know are unique in this business. I feel incredibly lucky to have this great opportunity. I try every day not to take these things for granted. Now, I'm still trying to figure out some of my potential. I'm trying to figure out how to use my background and blend into the film world. I'm still discovering a lot about film. Martial arts has definitely helped me with the disciplinary training, as you know, is so whacky and it's sometimes so dangerous. If you didn't have this kind of support that I have, this grounded foundation; I could see why so many people get caught up in it. They get so lost in this industry.

Chris Watson: Music was also a part of your childhood. Do you see any connection between the foundations of music and martial arts?

Chris Yen: Absolutely. They're both very rich art forms. It's an arena where you're allowed to express yourself. Especially with music, it's a universal language. I can see martial arts as being a universal language as well. I'm incredibly happy to see the way martial arts has come so far in the film business. To see that blend of culture with the film language and, of course, music makes all of that come alive. They all belong to the same family.

Chris Watson: You've also trained in acting. Tell me about some of your experiences outside of film. For instance, any training for acting or stage work.

Chris Yen: I'm still training for acting. It's not something you practice just a year or two and climb the ranks. It takes many, many, many years. Sometimes, my mom would say in the form of Tai Chi that something that looks so simple and so slow but it can take ten years just to master grasping that feeling of what it's like to be in that movement. As an actor, I would say it's the same thing. It takes years and years just to hone that kind of skill. Especially in Hollywood, it's such a difficult place with a pool of talented people. It's such a competitive market with so many undiscovered talents. You can't be in this business if you're not constantly training. I'm still training, going to my acting classes and work out at acting twice a week. I'm still out there auditioning. I treat an audition like I'm getting up on stage and doing my martial arts like when I was a kid. It's a performance, and I'm a performing artist; that's just what I do. I think acting has become a very involved, important part of my life. Now I can see there are other forms of expression that I can use. Also, it's a way to blend my martial arts background into acting. I'm still discovering that every time. A lot of people argue that martial artists never become serious actors. They can't be taken seriously as actors. There's no good acting that comes out of a martial artist. I can see where people are coming from with that, but I'm trying to discover acting within myself. I'm trying to prove that notion wrong. When you're very in tune with your body, with that level of training, it's not just a physical thing anymore. It's very psychological, it's very spiritual; I think great acting has to come from that. Personal life experiences from where you've been, what you've done, people in your life. It's a very deeply emotional thing for me when I talk about acting. I guess this is how I see it because I'm a martial artist. I really put it out there. I have so much appreciation for these great actors performing. It's a whole other kind of discipline in itself.

Chris Watson: How was your experience making *Close Encounter with a Vampire*?

Chris Yen: Wow, did you ever see that?

Chris Watson: I did. How old were you when you did that movie?

Chris Yen: I was very young. I was about nine. My experience on *Close Encounter with a Vampire*... let's say it was like being thrown into an ocean. I didn't know how to swim yet, but since my family gave me a really solid pair of flippers, I just paddled and kicked my way through. It was definitely the first taste of old Hong Kong filmmaking. I would describe that as being in boot camp—it was solid, military training. It was much like my martial arts training. I was incredibly fortunate to have that experience at an early age with a master like Yuen Woo Ping. He was like the Steven Spielberg of Hong Kong. I was too young to know that at the time. It was a whole other level of experience on set. Especially, having the opportunity to work in Hollywood and American films, I always look back to that time. It was very difficult. I was taken out of school. Suddenly, I'm on a plane and then to a cemetery. I got off the plane to Taiwan, I didn't speak the language. Luckily, my mother was there with me. Next thing I knew I was being put in ratty clothes and had dirt all over my face, crawling around in a cemetery trying to eat a chicken. That was my first day on set. I got to work with a bunch of kids. Yuen Woo Ping was very demanding. I remember a lot of screaming on set. We worked around the clock. There was a few times where we worked for three days straight. I got to rest on and off on set, but it's not like Hollywood. It's not like you have a union. It's still like that to this day. That gave me the toughness to face what we have to face in the industry here.

Chris Watson: Were you interested in acting at that point?

Chris Yen: I have no clue. It was like training in my martial arts every day. I never questioned why I was doing it. I just did it. Doing it was just like training martial arts any other day, just in another place. That's what it was for me. I don't think I ever looked at it like, "Oh, this is acting? This is what I want to do." As soon as we finished, I was back to school. I was back to being a normal kid again. I didn't really get interested until much later when I started working on film production with my brother. I'm a late developer. I'm still discovering a lot of things about myself now.

Chris Watson: What did you learn from Yuen Woo Ping?

Chris Yen: I learned to respond immediately on set. When you're shooting on a low-budget action film and you don't have restrictions, you have to act and think immediately on your feet. Sometimes you don't even have to think, you just have to react. The training gave me that physical conditioning to where I could respond. I remember that very vividly because that sort of training, getting my feet wet for the first time on that level of an action film, later getting into *Johnny Tao* this experience was seen as a luxury. I actually have time to respond, time to sit down, I can look at the clock and see when we'll get off work. Yuen Woo Ping really pushed me hard. I felt like I was nine, going on fifteen. Every day was like that. There was a lot of commotion, a lot of screaming people, a lot of kids running around, and no time. You didn't even have time to put on your make up. That's what I remember in my head, "Action! Action! Action!" Also, "NG," meant "No good." He used "NG" a lot. I think we must have had forty takes on one kick. He needed me to get that guy right smack in the face in a very precise angle. Of course, I didn't understand why then. You have to set up the camera a certain way and get it into the frame. I felt really, really bad because I was a kid. What am I doing kicking this old man in the face? There were thirty-nine "NGs." Yuen Woo Ping is an amazing action director. I'm very fortunate that I got to work with the master.

Chris Watson: When we are first introduced to you in *The Black Rose*, you pummel two guys with nunchucks. What were your thoughts on the cartoonish depiction of an otherwise brutal scene?

Chris Yen: Cartoonish, definitely. I understood at the time that we were doing something very campy, very fun, and very cartoonish.

The environment on the set was like that every day. Everybody was laughing, having fun, and making jokes. It was great because it was a very fun-filled air. I expected the outcome was going to be very comedic and over the top. I actually enjoyed the result. It was a lot of work going into it because it was a last minute project. I only had a couple of weeks to prepare. At the time, they had just written that character in. She didn't exist prior. All I knew was that I would probably be working with nunchucks. I had never done nunchucks before that—it's not incorporated into the Wushu system. Of course, I turned to none other than Bruce Lee, the nunchuck master. For those two weeks I remember just fast forwarding that scene in *Game of Death* (1978). Every chance I had I would watch it over and over again. The challenge came the first day of the shoot. Donnie threw me two pair of nunchucks, which I hadn't trained for. That was an experience to work through that. I think I accomplished that and proved to my brother that I could do it.

Chris Watson: How much time did you have to prepare for your fight scenes?

Chris Yen: Maybe twelve days. I was actually in Hong Kong at the time, working in film production. Acting wasn't even near me. I met a producer and he wrote in that part. I happened to be in Hong Kong at the time and they were, "Let's put her in front of a camera. Let's do this." It was a campy, colorful film so it fit. It was after that where I really found my calling. That movie in particular, and the experiences that came out of it, just made me realize what I really wanted to do.

Chris Watson: Which was more challenging—the scenes with weapons or hand-to-hand combat?

Chris Yen: It depends on who you're fighting with. It depends on what the scene entails. When you don't have to carry something in your hand and worry about the extension of the movement, it's much easier. Weapons definitely add another dynamic to it. Sometimes it can be very challenging. It does take a lot of rehearsal and precision to be doing that kind of stuff in front of the camera. Sometimes it's very challenging when your fellow actor is not really trained as well. It's a balance. You have to find ways where you can connect, even through physical movement.

Chris Watson: Also, in *The Black Rose*, there's a great scene where it's revealed that the three of you—two women in a bikini and you in a schoolgirl's outfit are waiting on him. What were your thoughts when you first saw the set-up and what do you think of the final product?

Chris Yen: That's funny. That scene didn't particularly stand out to me as much as the nunchuck scenes. I do remember shooting that on the bridge. It was done in a few takes. We were outside and didn't spend a lot of time on that bridge. A lot of the choreography was done at the very last minute. Considering all of that, I have to be happy with the results. I couldn't ask for anything more. It is what it is. It's fun, over the top Hong Kong comedy. It just happens to have some chop socky movements. I wouldn't call *The Black Rose* a serious martial arts film or even a serious acting film.

Chris Watson: Intentional or not, the women are very strong and dominant in *The Black Rose*. What statement does this add to the film?

Chris Yen: It's funny because I never thought about it at the time. We're predominantly surrounded by women on this film. It's funny you mention it, because this film was codirected by Chun-Chun Wong. It was codirected by a woman so it definitely has a woman's touch. I hope it's a positive statement. Chinese women come in all forms and colors.

Chris Watson: I think of the era of Shaw Brothers films where someone like Cheng Pei Pei was the heroine of the film.

Chris Yen: I grew up watching a lot those films in Chinatown. At the time, we had three Chinese theaters. I think it was a beautiful, positive thing. Being a Chinese woman myself, to see a fellow Chinese sister

Photo courtesy of Chris Yen.

be in a lead movie and to play that kind of character; to be strong, to be empowering, and to be able to kick butt always gives me goosebumps. That is what I live for. My mother was the epitome of that kind of character. When I see women like that onscreen, it's like I see my own mother on screen. I see my background, my childhood, and my family. In essence, I relate to it a lot. I'm drawn to it. It's good and refreshing. It seems like women always get these sexy types of characters. I think these types of characters are a lot deeper than that. They don't just fight. They don't just empower, but they're strong. They also have a deeply rooted cultural background. As long as it's not always about selling bikini-clad women and wielding swords, I'm all for that too, but I don't want to always go into that whole stereotype. For me as an actor, I try to stay away from those types of characters. I want to do something that's different and reveals, especially Asian women, in a very positive light. We don't all do kung fu and when we do kung fu we don't have to do it in a bikini.

Chris Watson: On a similar note, what impact do you see a film with strong female characters having on society?

Chris Yen: Certainly strong female characters who are portrayed to people, especially young people, are characterized as strong role models that I think is very important. Particularly young people are getting affected by what they see in the media and on screen. I think it's important that they see that the leadership roles are not always occupied by men. Strong leaderships roles can be occupied by men or women in all forms of profession. As I was getting older, helping my mom at her dojo teach classes, I worked with a lot of kids in the community. I grew up as the baby so it was a shift for me to occupy the older sister role. The kids who came to my mom's school, I learned that it was very important to be a role model. Some of those kids were boys. In the beginning, building a relationship with them, I had to overcome that "Oh, so you're a girl? You're going to teach me kung fu?" It's really important for me, working with kids, to show it doesn't really matter that I'm a woman. There's a discipline and culture involved here. I want you to see that women can do these roles. We can fit into these shoes. Men can do martial arts. Women can also do martial arts. I think kids are where it all starts from. It's the younger generation who will be looking at my films. Hopefully, I will be able to be a good role model for young women, young Asian-American women, and young Asian-American kids.

Chris Watson: Do you feel expectations were higher for you on *The Black Rose* because you were working under your brother?

Chris Yen: I feel that expectations are always higher. People might have thought, "Oh, his sister is working on this project. She's going to get special treatment." It was not the case. If anything, I probably got the worst treatment. That was a challenge in itself. The expectations are always going to be there with my family background. It's something we have to live with. The bar is set really high. These are the levels of expectation and I have to meet them. I like these kind of challenges. That's what helps drive me to overcome and make it better. Expectations were high, but I definitely welcomed it.

Chris Watson: What have you learned from your brother?

Chris Yen: I know I'm very fortunate to have inspirational example set before me in my family. My brother has worked so hard in his career. He paved the road for a next generation of martial artists. I'd like to be included in that pool. It's something that I definitely recognize and don't want to take for granted. I learned that you just have to stay on a path, be tenacious, do not give up your training, do not forget your roots, and just keep doing what I do. I have to keep working with the gifts I've been given. I have to keep honing the skills and try to discover new and better ways to improve on them. He's set an example for me because he's been in this business so many years. We're so many years apart. I didn't grow up with him. I grew up watching him on screen. We're both trained by my mother. His career has had a lot of ups and downs, and what I admire the most is that he stuck through it. He worked through the times when it was very difficult, and he never gave up. He never gave up his artistry as a martial artist. On a technical level, after seeing what he does on set, I've learned a lot of those tools. I learned how to shoot certain action scenes, how to think, choreography, and how to incorporate the two together. From an action filmmaker perspective, I got a glimpse inside of that world. I'm fascinated by that and hope someday that I can direct. I would incorporate some of those tools into that.

Chris Watson: I interviewed a martial artist who had a very negative view of martial arts actors. What are your thoughts on the subject?

Chris Yen: We've seen it all. Actors are able to be trained and be put on camera like they're real martial artists. If I were to train for a role as a dancer, I would train just as hard as I did with my martial arts to be convincing and believable. I think it's a very rewarding experience for the actor. There's the movement of the physical body and there's the filmmaker directing, the choreographer, and where the camera is placed to capture those movements to bring it to a realistic level. As a martial artist, having that training practically since birth, it's a whole other level to grasp the movements. It's more believable if you're a martial artist. It's so sophisticated that the untrained eye can't tell what you're watching. I have worked with both real martial artists and non-martial artists, trying to do action. I know from my own experience that there's always going to be that one thing that sets it apart or makes it a little bit more. I've worked on both sides and don't want to disrespect those people. I see the differences and I've lived the differences. Having a good foundation and body movement with the sophistication of filmmaking these days, actors with good discipline can push themselves to that level of believability, but it's very subjective.

Chris Watson: Your role in *Give 'em Hell Malone* could almost be the same character as *The Black Rose*. Were you concerned about being typecast as a villain?

Chris Yen: You can't really get away from being typecast. The nunchuck girl is the lighter, happier, smaller version. The other is darker, sinister, and interesting version. I try to get myself out there and do things that are a little bit different for myself. I'm a pretty low-key person. I don't want to regret not taking an opportunity, but I also feel it's important for me not to step into something I might regret later. By the way, I had a really good experience working on *Give 'em Hell Malone*. It was an incredible experience to work with a genius like Russell Mulchaly and veteran actors like Thomas Jane and Ving Rhames. I'm very grateful for that. You know, this question has come up before. People look at them as very similar characters. One difference is that one talks and the other doesn't. We didn't have much of a full script on *The Black Rose*. With *Malone*, I was really driven by the character. I wanted to explore who she was and how she became that way. *The Black Rose* was just fun, getting to go to the playground and play with the kids. That's how I would describe the differences between those experiences. I really got to bring in some of my acting training and experiences into *Give 'em Hell Malone*. That was really exciting for me. Wow, I get to tap into a different side of my brain now, while still using some of my physical movements. It wasn't an action vehicle as much as a character driven piece. I had a lot fun discovering this character.

Chris Watson: Your introduction in *Give 'em Hell Malone* is a gruesome one. What were your thoughts on this?

Chris Yen: I giggled the whole way through. It's very hard not to. Okay, this is definitely going to be different. I wonder how audiences are going to look at Chris Yen after this? It's a challenge, fun, and I know I can do this role. I particularly liked playing that scene because it was so out there, dark, and creepy. It's so different from what people think a typical martial artist should do. It's not a martial arts movie type of character. It was completely different for me, so I was excited to get into that character and getting into that dark world. I was very excited to see the outcome of it. I don't mind grotesque and horror. I love to watch horror movies. Nothing really turns me off. I'm not afraid to see that kind of stuff. I welcome it.

Chris Watson: Where did the combination of innocence and wickedness derive from and what were your thoughts on these characteristics?

Chris Yen: I always think it's fun to be a blend of both vulnerability and this evil strength. It was a lot of fun. It's stuff we get to do in acting classes, creating all those characters, back story, and world. I got to blend into the stuff that I had been training and learning. It was like going to play on set every day. The experience gave me a lot of great memories.

Chris Watson: Your character is a bad ass until Thomas Jane surprises her with a head-butt. Her sobbing reaction negates the build-up. If you could have had control over her reaction, what would you have her do?

Chris Yen: I saw this character as very unpredictable. She was a little girl trapped inside an adult body. With this multiple personality disorder that was at times psychotic, at times completely innocent, and at times Shirley Temple-ish… the original script actually had a lot of Shirley Temple qualities. I still refer to her as the sinister, Asian, Shirley Temple. I would have liked to have had a fight scene with Thomas Jane in that bloody faced, broken nose. She's actually rather vain. She was hysterical about the head-butt because her nose was broken. She realized her hand was covered with blood and her face was distorted. She was freaking out because this character is also quite vain. She thinks she's right. She thinks she's beautiful. I would've wanted to see a fight happen between the two of them. I think it would be wildly over the top and funny. It might give the character a chance to show more of her movements because she's very playful and colorful. I wouldn't say she's a martial artist, but she

Chris Yen in *Give 'em Hell Malone.*
Photo courtesy of Chris Yen.

definitely picked up some skills. The action is just part of her colorful personality rather than her being a natural martial artist.

Chris Watson: Had you seen *Highlander* (1986) before you did the movie?

Chris Yen: I saw *Highlander* a long time ago. It's a cult classic. Russell is a genius with his visual sensibility. I wish we had more time to work on *Give 'em Hell Malone* because he would have made it that much better. He just needed a little bit more time to tighten up some things.

Chris Watson: When you did the Sundance selection *A Good Day to be Black and Sexy*, was it an intentional stretch away from action films?

Chris Yen: I am first and foremost a martial artist. Second, I'm also an actor. The actor in me, I try to do things that are going to be different, especially if it's different from the whole martial arts world because people expect that. They're going to expect me to just do action films. As an actor, I will never have a chance to stretch if I'm just going to stretch to that genre. It was an incredible opportunity, and I hope there will be more like that. It was a very fun role that I had a chance to do. It was sort of my first comedic role with lines. *The Black Rose* is a comedic role, but she didn't talk. My character in *A Good Day to be Black and Sexy* is this mischievous, conniving teenager that likes girls. She was just sort of a brat. I had a chance to bring out a little of that child in me to play that. I tried to have fun with it. With the training I had, my upbringing was very serious. It was very militant. Martial artists are serious people, for the most part. Sometimes, I would like to have something refreshing in that mode; I think you need that. How else are you going to stay sane? It's a very refreshing piece. I would love the chance to do more romance and comedy. It doesn't always have to be action. As an actor, those are type of challenges I seek.

Chris Watson: Which of the genres do you prefer doing the most?

Chris Yen: I guess it depends on my mood and where I'm at. Right now, I'm producing. I have to psyche myself and put my mind in a different place. Actors are very moody people. One day, I'll wake up and feel like kicking and punching. Next day, I might feel romantic. I want to do a scene like in *The Notebook* (2004). Sometimes I get in these little fantasies. I watch a lot of films and get inspired that way. Every day, I see a blend of the martial artist in me and things involving the actor in me. I try to find ways to put that into my daily life. I don't have one preference over the other. I want to do things that are different for me. I want to explore new things and avoid doing the same things over and over again. I want to stretch now as far as I can.

Chris Watson: In *The Adventures of Johnny Tao*, how much input were you able to give for the fight scenes?

Chris Yen: That film was a very special, collaborative effort. We had a great stunt coordinator, Marcus Young. He's worked on many big budget action films. In fact, the team we worked with came from many big budget films. *The Adventures of Johnny Tao* was a low-budget film. What made it really special is that everybody treated it no different from a big budget film. I think they actually treated it with respect. We had limited resources, limited time, but we knew exactly where we were positioning and what this was. Everyone was in the right mind frame and spirit. The director, Kenn Scott, comes from a martial arts background. He had his vision for the story and how the action was going to blend in. Kenn and Marcus had worked on many projects together prior. To create the choreography, they used something from all of the actor's background. They used the Wushu training from my background. My fellow costars, Matt, is a karate expert and another is a gymnast. They mapped out what skill set each actor would bring. They used that to incorporate their vision and try to play to our strengths. I remember they were always asking us questions, trying to find ways to incorporate what we could do. We had a few weeks of training before shooting so we would rehearse every other day for three weeks. Half of it we were rehearsing with the wires. They asked questions to make sure we didn't get hurt and to make sure it was the way we would get the best out of each other. It was very collaborative. Everyone was very open.

Chris Watson: Do you have a preference on how your fight scene is coordinated?

Chris Yen: It depends on who I'm beating up. I don't really have a preference on certain moves, but I'm a sword-wielding type of martial arts gal. When you put a sword in my hand, tell me what the scene is about and I understand a character, I start thinking about all these colorful images in my head. That sword becomes second nature to me—it becomes an extension of my arm. If you were to ask me if I have a preference for a certain weapon, I would certainly say sword and then I'd take nunchuck on the other hand. I've been into mixed martial arts. The Wushu gave me a very solid foundation to be able to explore other forms of arts. I've done just that. Now, I'm incorporating the mixed martial arts into my traditional foundation. I'm still trying to think of it in terms of choreography and film discipline. I'm heavily into this now since I'm producing my first project, so I have to think along these lines. I have these images in my head when I'm going through my script, and I see very hardcore, realistic, brutal, jaw breaking, bone breaking…that sort of impact and the choreography, but at the same time I'd like to mix it up with a bit of grace. I want the sword technique to be fancy but not over the top. For me, the Wushu system is a grounded form of martial arts. At the end of the day, I would like to get back to that. I'm not into flying and wire works, even though it can be beautiful. I want to hone into the basics and get back into real ground fighting and realistic action choreography.

Chris Watson: There's a kick you do that reminds me of a reverse "Rothrock Sting." When did you first discover you could do the kick and what did you do to perfect it? You performed it on film when you were nine…

Chris Yen: I just call it "kick that guy with a flying front kick." When *The Matrix* (1999) first came out, and I saw that kick by Moss, I said, "Hey! That's my kick! That's the Yuen Woo Ping kick!" Prior to *The Matrix*, I had not seen it anywhere else. Michelle Yeoh and Cynthia Rothrock might have done it, but prior to that I hadn't seen it in any Hollywood films. It's not like a certain kick, like a roundhouse or a jumping back kick. It came out of my Wushu training and stretching; my mom stretched me since age three. I was quite flexible. It wasn't like a kick you perfected for one project, but I think the flexibility gave me the ease in being able to deliver a kick like that for the camera. I would love to be able to do that kick again and get a little creative with it.

Chris Watson: Have you ever tried the "Rothrock sting?"

Chris Yen: Yeah, actually. When I was younger and my back didn't have so many injuries, I had a very flexible back. I was able to jump up in the air and do a double back kick and touch my head. I might have been the first person to do that. I haven't seen that yet—double, jumping, back kick to the head.

Chris Yen performs double back kick.
Photo courtesy of Chris Yen.

Chris Watson: You've done some fight choreography. Is that also going to be an interest of yours?

Chris Yen: I don't see myself pursuing a lot of work as an action choreographer, but because of my background and being involved with action films, any sort of action film I'm going to be involved with is going to involve and incorporate that knowledge and language. I have those tools; why not use them? It actually benefits me to go into a project with that kind of knowledge. I would want to use that knowledge to the best of my ability. I don't see myself becoming a choreographer as a career, but there will always be a space for me to incorporate the choreography in any action film I do.

Chris Watson: What do you believe makes a strong, female character?

Chris Yen: Wow, there's so many ways to answer that. I want to throw you fifty different answers, so I'm going to try to pick just one. The obvious is confidence. Also, belief in truth. Whether or not you're a martial artist doesn't matter. I think those are very important aspects—confidence, truth, belief.

Chris Watson: Who would you consider to be a Bad Ass Women of Cinema and why?

Chris Yen: There's so many. I think of strong actors, like Nicole Kidman and Naomi Watts. I don't believe it always has to be a woman in action films. Since we are on that subject, Michelle Yeoh would definitely be one. She's set the precedent and paved the road for people like me. She is in her true form and a martial artist. She's not just some dancer but a trained martial artist. Natalie Portman, especially her portrayal in *Black Swan* (2010). It's a character I found very heartfelt and enduring. It's about artistry. I saw my own mother when I watched the film. Of course, it's on a whole different level. The fact that the movie shows what it takes. Any artist would feel for what is underlying in that film. It's about perfection, improving it, and doing it until it's perfect. I've watched Natalie Portman's career growing up. She was a young starlet and most of them don't get to sustain a career in this industry. She's one of the few that has. Natalie seems like a very grounded woman. To have her success, it's not by chance or luck but with the variety of roles she's played I can relate to her. She has a dream career that any actress would love, but I see a lot of discipline behind that. As a martial artist, we know that's what it takes. Definitely Cheng Pei Pei—I grew up watching her films. A lot of people thought my mom and Cheng Pei Pei looked alike. Whenever I see Cheng Pei Pei it brings images of my mom. She's a screen icon.

LADY TERMINATOR:
A LOOK BACK

SELDOM CAN ONE ROLE DEFINE SOMEONE'S CAREER, BUT THAT'S THE case with Barbara Anne Constable. Barbara played the lead in *Lady Terminator*, blowing away male genitalia with a vengeance. The Indonesian film was a box-office smash before being banned. The film garnered word of mouth from websites and magazines, building the movie's popularity. For instance, Jose Prendes of StrictlySplatter.com wrote, "there will never (ever, ever) be another movie on StrictlySplatter.com that tops the insanity from start to finish that this amazing movie manages to pull off with flying colors. Constantly hilarious and entertaining, this is a shining example of bad movies (which works in its favor) making it a pure and undeniable work of art." *Lady Terminator* amassed such a following

Lady Terminator Poster

that the movie continues to screen in an abundance of packed theaters worldwide. The film is memorable for its use of sex, violence, knock-off plot points, and unique afterlife, all of which can be viewed through the eyes of its unknown star.

Barbara was born in London, England, but grew up in Brisbane, Australia. As a child, her main focus was dancing. Barbara experienced "a lot of domestic violence and alcohol issues" over the course of her childhood. At fifteen, Barbara began modeling, getting her start in bridal magazines. Eventually, modeling led to acting. Before landing her landmark role, the modeling led to a bit role in a Hong Kong movie. Due to an injury, Barbara would visit modeling agencies in Hong Kong. One agent would submit her for a film that would become *Lady Terminator*. Barbara would audition and receive the role. Barbara said, "I was just modeling. I had some acting experience, but could never afford to be an actor. The role didn't require a lot of speaking, but did require a lot of physical endurance. I had to look a certain way, and was very fit." Perhaps the biggest hurdle for any actress interested in the role was the nudity and violence.

In terms of the nudity involved with *Lady Terminator*, Barbara was more than comfortable. As a model, she appeared in an overseas version of *Penthouse*. On nudity, Barbara stated:

> I always had a freedom with my body. I never had an issue with being in the nude. We're born in the nude. When you're dancing, you're in leotards and short-shorts and little tops. You're constantly rehearsing with next to nothing on anyway. Everybody around you is the same. When you're doing shows, you have so many costume changes within a two hour show that you're ripping your clothes off and running around with no clothes on, so is everybody else. You become accustomed to it. That's part of it. Also, I think it's

because athletes have incredible bodies. They know they look good and don't feel self-conscious about their body.

The nudity would not be an issue for Barbara. The flawless nudity would make the movie all the more memorable, but the heavy violence steals the show.

With the high level of violence comes the need to use weapons, but the star of the film had never fired a gun before. Barbara says, "When I first arrived, they gave me a workshop. It was an Army guy that showed me how to load, reload, shoot, target, aim, and fire. When you fired, you really had to have a good hold of it. Otherwise, it knocked you around. That's the only time I ever shot guns before or since." After training, the star of the film began blowing away men.

The violence played a strange role in not only the movie but also Barbara's personal life. In response to the violence, Barbara stated:

> I've had a lot of anger toward men. I still do have the anger. I wrote a book on domestic violence when I came back from Hong Kong in my twenties. My first serious relationship from about age 19 to 25 was with a guy who started beating me up. When I did Lady Terminator, it was easy for me to do because it was a cathartic experience for me. It helped me to kill all these men. I was able to get rid of all that rage, and do it in a safe way. There's definitely a lot of anger and rage that I directed in that character. That's why it was so easy for me to play that character.

Although the movie was a "joke" to the lead actress, she was able to wrestle with her demons and gladly take her $30,000 paycheck. The memorable violence may have been therapeutic for its star but many of the ideas stemmed from another film.

Many film fans will mention *Lady Terminator* is a female starrer that borrows heavily from *The Terminator* (1984). While enough is changed in the stories, to name a few notable similarities is not difficult. For instance, both films include the quiet killer at the helm, the mass killing scene, and the infamous eyeball scene. At the time, the knock off concept was not unusual. 1983's *Hundra* featured Laurene Landon as a female Conan character. Both *Hundra* and *Lady Terminator* had a Roger Corman and, later, Asylum Entertainment knock-off schlockiness to them, but they become something special by switching the lead to a female. With any female action hero comes the discussion of feminism. These two films are prime examples of how Hollywood saw female action heroes. The Hollywood studio versions each feature a masculine male. The independent films feature women. Having a female lead is just one reason why *Lady Terminator* is considered a feminist statement.

Lady Terminator seems filled with attempts at feminism. For instance, the majority of the kills involve crotch violence, prompting many to consider the violence a heavy handed feminist statement. The film, especially the first half, is littered with phallic symbols. When asked about all the symbols, Barbara recognized the significance, stating, "The big erect cock is the symbol of manhood. I suppose in the film it was masculinizing me. The power of the cock was transferred to me. I was having their cocks ripped off, shooting them off. The symbolism is wrapped up in that." However, the symbolism and creative deaths were not all in the script. Instead, they came from the mind of director H. Tjut Djalil. The film became about obliterating the men. Barbara says the male directed violence "wasn't so much in the script as in the direction. He wanted those deaths to be brutal." Djalil uses a similar style in his other films. Also, there's even the classic line, "I'm not a lady. I'm an anthropologist." While the line gets laughs in theaters for its over the top nature, it has a lot more to say than what's on the surface. When asked about the quote, Barbara replied, "I think what she was trying to say was, 'Don't call me lady because I'm not. I'm not a vagina. I'm a true professional. Just because I'm female, you keep calling me lady. I'm actually an educated woman.' It's again about a woman standing up for her rights and equality." In the film, the well-educated woman would eventually become possessed, and the raging crotch violence would begin. Barbara "relate(d) to her shooting the cocks off. The correlation for me is that a strong woman killing men, shooting their cocks off, is what a lot of women really wish they could do to certain men." Whether you're looking at feminism as equality for all or women conquering all, this film has it.

The star of the film would do her best to forget the film that personally "empowered" her. Like many actors from cult films, the movies get hidden away and, often, forgotten. A good example can be seen in a story filmmaker Jack Hill told during an interview. He ran into an actor a few years after they worked together. The actor was very embarrassed by the movie they made together. Twenty years later, the movie is a cult hit. Jack goes to a convention and sees the actor selling photos from the movie. Likewise, Barbara thought *Lady Terminator* was "fucking crap" and looked "amateur" when she first saw it. Despite the box office success, even the star's copy of the film was stored away and forgotten. Unfortunately, the film was banned in Indonesia and seemed lost. Barbara never thought the movie would be seen again, let alone become a cult classic. Luckily, the movie continues to be seen at midnight showings and revived releases. With its success has come its acceptance from the star. She has shown the film to her family and friends, has accepted numerous interviews, and has appeared at *Lady Terminator* events. The over-the-top violence, bad acting, and dialogue is comical in its absurdity.

When a viewer is able to accept that, you get an addictive, trashy treat.

INDEX

ABOUT THE AUTHOR

Chris Watson has written for *Black Belt Magazine*, *Inside Kung-Fu Magazine*, *Classic Images*, and numerous other magazines. He also cowrote the books *Reflections on Blaxploitation*, *Joe Estevez: Wiping Off the Sheen*, *Dwarfsploitation*, and more. Most recently, he wrote the introduction for the book *Gods of the Grindhouse*. He has both a B.S. degree in Elementary Education and M.A. in English.

Contact: WriterChrisWatson@gmail.com

www.ingramcontent.com/pod-product-compliance
Lightning Source LLC
Chambersburg PA
CBHW060334100426
42812CB00003B/986